# QUEEN OF HARTS

# Queen of Harts

LASHAUN KEMP

Dedicated to my mama Vickie, the strongest and most beautiful woman that I've ever known. Your love and dedication to your family will never be forgotten. Thank you for pouring so much of yourself into me. As a woman and a mother I see and understand the sacrifices that you made to push your family forward. Thank you for showing me how to love, nurture, and stand firm in my faith. I hope to always make you proud. I love you forever and always.

~ 1 ~

QUEEN OF HARTS

By:

LaShaun Kemp


## Chapter 1

A barely stable Jacquelyn walked towards the cobble steps leading to the iron-framed door. The familiar sounds of sirens racing past the neighborhood matched the continuous ringing in her ears. All of the crying and screaming at the funeral had nearly deafened her. Yet, sound, or the lack there of, didn't faze her. As Jacquelyn entered the house, the same script-like condolences she received at the funeral were on repeat the minute she stepped through the door. Looking into their sad eyes, she need not listen as she could read their lips and knew exactly what they would say. "I'm sorry, baby. If you need ANYTHING, call me," was the most popular phrase. She'd nod her head and wait for the next mourner to approach with the same line with a slight variation. Some mourners chose to stand out more than others. The same ones who would barely wave or say hello now seemed *heartbroken, yet those with the loudest cries. For instance, Mrs. Herd, a next-door neighbor who would switch sidewalks to avoid speaking to you for all to witness, chose this day to make the pulpit into her personal stage. While others simply walked to the front to place a flower on the casket, she pleaded with the Lord.*

*"Jesus, no! It ain't right! Help us, Father!" wailed Mrs. Herd, after she walking to the casket, stretching her hands to the Heavens and falling to her knees. She continued with her one-woman production for two more minutes until she was cut short by the answer to her questions. "Why not me? Take me, Lord! Take me!" she wailed.*

*"Yes, take her, Lord," yelled a random voice.*

*With that response, Mrs. Herd's cry went from loud wailing to a soft whimper as she pulled herself together and staggered to her feet. There was as much peace as a funeral could provide for a few minutes. That is until the day's outstanding performance came from Uncle Davis' wife, Shirley. She burst through the double doors clasping a single rose and screaming,*

*"Lord, no! Why, Lord, why? I wasn't ready for this." Her outburst was followed by a few deep gasps as she crumbled onto the floor, kicking her feet and pounding her fists against the carpet floor like a spoiled child.*

*Jacquelyn heard one of the deacons' murmurs, "This woman lost her dignity right along with her mind."*

*But as soon as she noticed that her dress was beginning to wrinkle, she sustained herself. If all eyes were going to be on her, she did not want anything to be out of place. Uncle Davis* trailed behind her and steered her to her seat in a nearby pew as she continued her scene. She rocked herself to a steady rhythm while the organist began softly playing, all while the attention remained on her. Leapt from her seat, waived her arms, and then rose, causing some petals to fall. She tried to begin crying out again but was fortunately cut short as the choir started to sing while drowning out her gibberish. Still, Shirley wasn't ready to let go of the limelight. She joined the chorus singing Amazing Grace.

"How sweet the sound, yes it was, mm-hmm, so sweet."

She sang every key but the right one. Her performance ended after Uncle Davis had had enough and carried her out before the minister spoke the final words.

"All of this, and she hasn't even called in over three years," Jacquelyn whispered to herself.

Jacquelyn let the door to the house swing open, at first a little hesitant to walk in alone. Then she assured herself,

I won't be alone for too long. Everyone will be here in a while after they finish at the site. Then they can help me clear up all this food... "What do they expect us to do with all of this?" She spoke aloud as she looked around at the endless food given to them by various family members, friends, and old acquaintances.

Jacquelyn's focus lingered between brokenhearted family and friends to this surplus of casseroles, cakes, and pies. However, bittersweet memories always seemed to break any type of temporary focus. Jacquelyn's concentration was drawn away by the assortment of pictures throughout her grandmother's living room. She looked at each photo, some on the fireplace *mantle, encased decoratively. Others were scattered on the coffee table, taken from photo albums the night before. The most vivid images were forever captured in her mind. For a moment, she smiled, thinking of one. Nevertheless, seconds later, she was again immersed in sorrow and tears. Those tears that she had waited for finally began to fall. The first two trailed from each eye down her cheeks and were followed by a steady flow. She had felt cold for not shedding even a tear since the initial loss. The hurt was there with or without the tears. Still, to Jacquelyn, it confirmed that she could express some type of emotion, even if no one could witness it. She did not need an audience. She felt everyone was waiting for her to react, but she couldn't share in their open display of grief. It made her feel too exposed. She now gasped overcome from the emotions she couldn't bottle any longer.*

*From the moment of the loss, she had severed her emotions, hoping it would save her from the pain. With everyone else around, she told herself that she had to keep it together. That's how they usually saw her, and that's how she needed them to see her. Jacquelyn met her nightmare as she knelt beside the solid coffee table and slowly slid to the cold wooden floor. This young woman's nightmare was simply being alone. Oddly, she didn't know whether to feel relief or sadness. She felt both, relief because she had faced something* she had repeatedly struggled against and sadness because her worst nightmare had come true.

In such a short time, Jacquelyn had lost her best friend and someone who had long ago become her will to go on. Her anchor had all but faded.

"Pathetic," said Jacquelyn when she saw her reflection on the blank television screen. Stumbling to the bathroom to better view herself, more tears blurred her vision.

Usually, when she walked, it was more like a glide, as if she were in a room of subjects and all must recognize her presence. Jacquelyn's famous walk gained her the nickname Queen, given to her by her grandmother Lena. At the same time, her demeanor was always humble. Her long, thick, black hair framed her sweet face that rarely went without a smile. During this moment, her walk turned into an aimless stride. It was as if someone had suddenly pushed her off of her throne. She turned on the light switch. The old light fixture flickered on and off, then stayed on to reveal a clearer image of a tear-stained face in the mirror. Jacquelyn held on to the porcelain sink as she peered into the mirror. She searched through her reflection's eyes, almost searching for "Jacquelyn," which wasn't uncommon for her. It was a ritual she had faithfully performed since her childhood. To many, it would be like a game of mirror-mirror, like in Snow White, except no one appeared to give her the answers.

"What do I do?" she asked the reflection, almost waiting for a response.

"Only God knows, baby. You can't find it all in yourself, Queen," her grandmother Lena would say when she would see

*Jacquelyn, staring into the mirror. Lena would continue, saying, "When will you learn? You've been doing that since you were knee-high and still haven't gotten any further."*

*Her earlier utterance of the word pathetic was not entirely directed toward her reflection, but to the situation and what she had allowed it to do to her.*

*"Supposed to be the Queen," she muttered.*

*Far from it, she thought. She shook her head in shame over her image while walking from the bathroom into the narrow hallway. The shades limited the amount of sunlight in her room, almost symbolizing the different circumstances in her life. Too many times Jacquelyn had allowed her problems to shade and block out the happiness in her life. She settled on the creaking bed as more tears rolled off her face, listened to the clock ticking on her knight stand, and caught her breath as the emotions grabbed her by the throat. Her only desire was to sleep and forget, clutching her old stuffed tiger wishing he could bring the same comfort he had brought her years ago as a child. She closed her eyes tightly, hoping for darkness only to find memories. Jacquelyn couldn't find solace even in her own room, so she retreated to the safest place she always could. From the time she could remember, Jacquelyn knew she could find comfort in her grandmother's room. Lena's door was open to all of her grandchildren, but especially to her dear Jacquelyn. She and her granddaughter shared a close bond. Around everyone else, Jacquelyn felt the need to display her independence, which caused those around her to rely on her. The room smelled like warm vanilla and jasmine, it smelled like Lena. Jacquelyn breathed in deeply hoping to lock every note of the scent in her mind.*

*After her parents died that's one of the first things that faded from her memories, their scent. Jacquelyn had a head scarf that belonged to her mother. She would secretly bury her face into the silk scarf until eventually her scent grew too faint to recognize. The lost scent created another wave of grief that rushed over a young Jacquelyn. It was one of the last pieces of her mother that made the loss feel final. As children Jacquelyn and her brother Deon lost their parents to a car accident. With such an early loss in her young life Jacquelyn was always afraid that she would end up entirely alone. Lena seemed to be the only one who knew the depth of her granddaughter's pain. Lena was the only person she could trust to open up to without the need to display the facade of constant strength. With her grandmother Jacquelyn could expose even the weakest parts of herself. Jacquelyn opened the door to Lena's room to find open photo albums and loose pictures sprawled about on her bed. Funny, she thought, this bed always looked much bigger, remembering nights when she would sneak into her grandmother's bed after a bad dream.*

*While moving a few photo albums away and pushing a few letters aside to make a spot for herself, she noticed a smaller book, unlike the others. It held the engraved title Diary of Lena Hart. Without a second thought, Jacquelyn opened it to the first page, dated March 22, 1978, about a year before darkness began to creep into her family's life. She had always wished she could read Lena's mind, and this was the next best thing. Besides, there was no one there to object.*

*Chapter 2*

*It's a shame what this neighborhood is coming to. I look out the window, and of course, somebody's walking up and down the sidewalk, but I can't help but wonder what's happening in that somebody's mind. Does anyone see the same thing I do when I look around? The streets my children played in are now marred by yellow tape and chalk outlines. I see the ghost of a place many of us built our dreams around. Nothing but misguided souls cloud my vision of what once was. You can't pass the market store up the street without seeing some girl strolling up and down the same block like she's waiting for a bus. These girls are one and the same, only with a different faces and back story. Most are barely old enough to purchase alcohol, yet they sell their souls to the highest bidder. I'm just blessed that I've never had to pull one of my girls from the side of the road. It would break my heart to see any of my kin out there. Not to mention safety in your driveway, or the lack of it. Like the other night, I left my car in my driveway, and the following day I found a dent the size of a baseball on the passenger side. I'd like to think it came from a stray baseball from the kids playing around. But I take pride in all of my possessions, especially that car. It was my Vic's first brand-new car. It would break his heart to see it the way it is. I can only imagine what he'd say about this neighborhood. He'd probably question why I stayed here this long. This is where we raised our family. Too many memories still live here to just leave them behind. I just can't seem to tear myself away from this old house. When I go through our closet, I get a whiff of his cologne from the suit of his that I kept. I miss him so much, but I see him daily in Jacquelyn. Queen is so much like that man; it's scary sometimes. It's like he left a piece of himself in each of his children and grandchildren. Deon looks like him, but Jacquelyn acts just like her grandfather. I laugh at times just at the things she'll say. That's my baby.*

*Lena, a classic beauty in her own right, had no grievances with time. Where wrinkles and saggy skin should be, tight and resilient toffee-tinted skin peeked through colorful house coats and dresses. Jacquelyn smiled at what her grandmother had written about her. She remembered the car incident, too. Yet, she knew the reason behind the "baseball dent". If Lena had looked a little closer, she would have noticed that her car wasn't even parked the way she had left it the night before. Jacquelyn knew who was behind the whole thing. She could picture it all as she let her memory take her back to the night before her grandmother's prized possession was damaged by default. Earlier that day, Deon tried to be on Lena's good side to get to her car but landed on the opposite end. His angelic eyes almost made up for his occasional wicked ways. He took pride in his barely visible chin hair, making his face seem slightly more mature. The rest of his missing facial hair gave him a boyish appeal, but he quickly reminded anyone that he was a grown man. Even though Jacquelyn was in her room making her bed, she could hear Deon's loud mouth.*

*"Come on, grandma."*

*"I just don't know, baby. Your Aunt Gwen needs to use it tomorrow to pick up her boy and your Uncle Ray from the train station."*

*"But what does tomorrow have to do with tonight?" Deon pleaded as he tried to keep his facade of patience.*

*"I just know how you are about putting gas back in the car. Remember a couple of Sundays ago? As a matter of fact, it was the first Sunday and the day before I let you use my car. Gwen went to crank the car up for me, and the hand was on E. We would have missed service if Mrs. Hill hadn't been running late for church, but I don't think it would have bothered you because you were still asleep. Bless your heart," she said with as much sarcasm as possible.*

*By this time, Jacquelyn had made her way from the creaky wooden floors of the hallway to the kitchen to add her two cents to the conversation.*

*"Hey, grandma, what does he want now?" she questioned as if she hadn't heard a word they had said.*

*Standing behind the other side of the counter, Deon completely ignored his sister's presence, remaining focused* on winning over his grandmother. However, Lena's attention shifted to Jacquelyn when her feet hit the kitchen floor.

"Morning Queen." She beamed as she gave her a kiss on the cheek.

"So, I'm invisible now, right? Everybody, the Queen has arrived!" He announced and proceeded to clap, mocking his sister's name.

"Now, can we get back to the business?" Gwen came around the corner before he could get a word from Lena.

"Boy, the only business you need to be worrying about is how you're gonna fix that bathroom light. You were supposed to get to it last week. How am I supposed to get my face together in the morning with that light going on and off every two minutes?" She paused, grinning, "But maybe it's not too bad. Some people say I look like Pam Grier in a dimly lit room. Kinda' nice to start your day off looking like that," she said, tossing her honey-brown hair.

"Who told you that, Sid the drunk? Well, maybe I need to take care of that light. I don't need another "star" walking around here," said Deon as he pinched Jacquelyn. Gwen thought of herself as Ms. Grier's lookalike. While they had similarities, and although she was a beautiful woman, her nephew had no problem bringing her back to reality.

"Well, let's make a deal, baby. If you fix that bathroom light, we can talk about me handing you those keys", said Lena, interjecting between the two.

"Okay, consider it done. I don't need the car till later on anyway. That should give me enough time to handle some other business," he said as he left the kitchen, along with his concern for the bathroom light.

"You better remember your business here too," yelled Gwen to an oblivious Deon. As soon as he touched the front porch, he was deaf to his aunt's words.

"As much running around as that boy does, you'd think he'd be a track star by now. The only reason he comes home is to rest and eat. Sort of reminds me of my husband."

"Gwen, don't be so hard on him. That man works harder than anyone I know. I think that's why your Daddy liked him so much," said Lena, speaking on her son-in-law's behalf.

"Yeah, but Daddy knew when to give up on something before it consumed everything he built. All that hard work and I return home with a husband and a child. At my age, I'm back home, at the age of..." she paused. "At the age of twenty-nine." she said, winking at Jacquelyn. Jacquelyn remained silent the entire time Lena and Gwen went back and forth, allowing the two women to handle their own dispute.

"Don't worry baby, all of them aren't like this," said Lena to Jacquelyn. "This?" questioned Jacquelyn. "Married women. Look at me. You don't see me bad-mouthing my husband, do you?"

"That's because he's been dead for six years." Gwen just laughed and shook her head. She knew she couldn't win against her Mother. After her last comment, Gwen didn't mind letting her Mother have the final word. "Don't take this one as an example of all of us," she said while tapping Gwen on her cheek. "Just make sure you know what you're getting into, Queen."

"By the way both of you are talking, people would think I'm getting married tomorrow." Lena looked at Jacquelyn up and down. "The way you and Will act, you'd think that was the case."

"Far from it!" responded Jacquelyn.

"Ha! That's what I said," added Gwen. The conversation ended with the short ding of the doorbell.

"You hear that sound? Those are the only bells I want to hear right now. No wedding bells in the meantime" added Jacquelyn. Gwen made her way to the door and peered through the peephole. She grinned and turned her head away from the door before answering it.

"Someone's ears must have been burning the whole way here." She dramatically threw the door open to reveal the visitor. "Will, how are you, honey? Seems to me you're doing well by the looks of things," she said without giving him a chance to answer. "Come on in," she said as she eagerly pushed the young man into the room.

Jacquelyn rolled her eyes at her aunt's unnecessary acting skills. Yet, Will had encountered Gwen's path enough times to know how to deal with her.

"I'm good, Gwen, maybe not as good as Ray, but I'm getting by." Just mentioning her husband's name caused Gwen to clear the room in ten seconds flat.

Left with nothing more to say except,

"Try not to have Queen out too late," she smiled slightly and swiftly walked by Will with her defaulted ego trailing behind.

Gwen wondered if everyone knew her business. Jacquelyn had to have told him. How else would he have known? She passed Jacquelyn, rolled her eyes, and murmured, "Don't let anyone else's dirty laundry slip out of your mouth any time soon, especially when you got stains of your own."

"What's wrong with her now," wondered Jacquelyn.

Will met Jacquelyn's eyes with a smile. Behind the sweet smile, she knew his mission was accomplished. Gwen had cleared the room taking her intentions of prying along with her. Will had a smile that would get him out of any argument with Jacquelyn. It was complimented by his charming way with words. Of course, when dealing with a woman like Jacquelyn, any man had to have a way with their words.

The couple left for a day in the park. Will's Impala eased into the parking spot as he started an unwanted conversation. She knew he would be on her case about her attending his parent's anniversary dinner. Before Will parted his lips to speak, Jacquelyn could guess how the conversation would go.

*His words would fall like raindrops a little at a time until finally, Jacquelyn found herself in a complete thunderstorm. Jacquelyn didn't mind being around Will's parents; besides their high social status, they were pretty regular. They even seemed taken by Jacquelyn's charming manor, looking beyond her family's social status. However, Jacquelyn felt entirely out of place regarding specific gatherings such as this one. Among the company of their posh friends, his parents, Mr. and Mrs. Jacobs, never adopted the same superior attitude, but their guest ensured Jacquelyn knew she did not belong. At these times, Jacquelyn caught herself constantly reading between the lines. If one of Mrs. Jacobs' friends gave her a compliment, she would examine every aspect, including their intentions behind the compliment. One thing always meant another with this crowd. The women in their circle smiled at their prey, shooting darts from their eyes and razors with their tongues. Mrs. Jacobs' friend Mrs. Smith could simply say,*

*"Jacquelyn, you look amazing in that dress. You know Mrs. Walker's daughter has one similar to that one, but on you, it's gorgeous. You wear it so well. You must have gotten it from that same place. I didn't know you shopped on Baker Street!" She'd smile as her girlfriends studied Jacquelyn. Translation: "Seen it before, not impressed, and can you really afford a dress like that on your salary?"*

*Will interrupted her flashback.*

*"I know I've already asked you, but before you give me a solid no, just listen. I already see that you have your mind made up about my parent's friends. Their opinions mean nothing.*

*My parents love you, and even if they felt differently about you, it wouldn't matter because I want you there."*

*"I know, but it turns into one big performance for me. I just feel out of place. I mean, I know that's how they see me anyway, out of place."*

*"Maybe if you didn't allow your own insecurities to get in the way, you could learn how to enjoy yourself. You're the main one putting yourself under a magnifying glass. Everybody around you sees you as perfect!"*

*"If they only knew, huh!" quipped Jacquelyn.*

*"Yeah!" was all he could add. Jacquelyn sat still, arms folded and head turned away from Will. He could see that he was quickly losing ground with Jacquelyn. Being the less stubborn one, Will proceeded. Taking a deep breath, he continued,*

*"Look, I didn't bring you out here to upset you. We can leave the entire subject alone." He nudged her arm, and she gave in. If it was choice between an afternoon laden with back and forth conversations over the Jacobs' friends or a literal stroll in the park, Jacquelyn would easily choose the ladder. She knew Will was in her corner no matter the opposition, but she also understood his family maintaining appearances with their inner circle was of high value to them. Both Mr. and Mrs. Jacobs came from humble beginnings, building their wealth together and joining a class that had shunned them only a few decades prior came with several stigmas that each family member put efforts forth to shake. Will was not the exception. They were coined as new money and no amount of fancy dinners, generous donations or brunches with the*

other wives of high society could erase that, but that wouldn't keep the Jacobs' from trying.

Later that night is when the whole "dent incident" took place. Jacquelyn had just opened the front door to the house, but before she could get both of her feet into the doorway, Deon was yet again trying to make his way out of the house.

"Where are you going?" asked Jacquelyn. "Everyone else is asleep. What are you trying to get into?"

"You got your life, and I got mine. If it's okay with you, Queen, we can keep our business separate. You've been gone all day. You don't see me interrogating you." Jacquelyn heard the jingling of keys as he pushed her aside.

"I hope you don't think you're leaving anywhere with Grandma's car. You know if she..."

Deon interrupted her.

"This is between me and Grandma, alright, Queen. Everything that goes on under this roof doesn't concern you. Good night." He walked away briskly, but not before giving her a sloppy wet kiss on her cheek. He'd done it since they were kids after he won an argument or had the last word just to antagonize his sister.

"I wouldn't crank the car up in the driveway if I were you," she said while wiping off her damp cheek.

Those were the only pieces of advice she could give him as he slowly closed the door. Simply saying Don't go wouldn't keep him from walking out the door. Besides, she didn't feel like hearing Aunt Gwen and Grandma that night. Jacquelyn knew if either of them woke up to Deon taking off, no one would get rest that night. With both of their mouths combined, the whole neighborhood would lose sleep. She could see that her brother had taken her advice. Jacquelyn watched from the living room window. Deon eased the car out of the driveway. He'd taken the emergency break-off and cautiously coasted down the street.

"At least he listens to me sometimes," said Jacquelyn to herself.

"Maybe he should do it more often," said a familiar voice. Jacquelyn turned around to see whom the voice belonged to.

"Uncle Ray!" she said, still trying to speak in a pitch a little above a whisper.

"Hey baby girl, I see you still try to watch after that brother of yours."

"Yeah, someone has to. How have you been?" Jacquelyn already knew the answer to that. Aunt Gwen talked about it every chance she got, and everyone knew that, including her own husband. Ray couldn't catch a break with Gwen. He laughed. Ray knew his wife had no qualms about sharing his shortcomings with anyone who would listen.

"Well, I'm here," he said, throwing his hands up. "I'll fill you in on the rest in the morning. Right now, both of us need to get some shut-eye. We can't all be night owls like Deon."

*Jacquelyn shook her head in agreeance, and hugged her uncle goodnight before parting down the hallway.*

*The night owl of the family had barely left the nest for a few hours when Jacquelyn was awakened by her brother shaking her from a sound sleep.*

*"Jacquelyn, you sleep?" she snatched his hands from her shoulders.*

*"I would be if you weren't shaking me like a rag doll. Boy, this better be good for you to be waking me up at...." She grabbed her clock to check the time. "2:12 in the morning!"*

*"It is important. I just need you to look at something for me." Jacquelyn scrunched her face as she rose from the bed and followed her brother. Deon was always getting into something. She now wondered what this something could be.*

*They crept through the dark hallways and eased down the old wooden steps, carefully stepping over the creaky ones. Over time they had memorized which ones creaked and which ones didn't so that they could sneak in and out without stirring Lena or anyone else from their sleep. All of the Hart children learned how to dodge the old steps that acted as an alarm for Lena. Deon opened the front door.*

*"Why are we going outside?" asked Jacquelyn.*

*"Because that's the only way you can see it."*

*"I hope, for your sake, it has nothing to do with Grandma's car!" Deon turned his head and walked through the door with his sister trailing behind him, failing to acknowledge his sister's words. He led her to the front end of the driver's side of the car. Jacquelyn laid her eyes on the orange-sized dent. The moon light showed just a fraction of how deep the*

indention truly was. Jacquelyn stared blankly. Her reaction fell short of what Deon expected. She always had at least one or two choice words regarding this. She stood there contemplating. Jacquelyn knew how much that car meant to their grandmother. To Lena, it wasn't simply a car. It represented the hard work that she and her husband had put forth. Their grandparents stood on the merit of paying cash for everything they owned. It had taken their grandfather years to purchase that car for Lena and with

"Queen, it's not that bad, is it? I mean, it's not like I crashed it. It's noticeable, but...." He trailed off not even believing his own words.

Jacquelyn finally spoke, asking, "How?"

Deon sighed and then began. "Well, you know Charlene's Daddy has a quick temper. I took her out and brought her home a little late." He put a strong emphasis on the word little.

"How late?" questioned Jacquelyn speaking through her teeth.

"About ten minutes ago." Jacquelyn just shook her head in disbelief. Deon returned to his explanation. She shifted positions, kneeling to get a better view of the damage.

Deon continued his explanation, "I'm walking her to the door, and then the next thing I know, her Daddy is chasing me with a bat down their steps. I jumped in the car. He was aiming for me, but he missed."

"I can see that!" shrieked Jacquelyn. She didn't know whether to slap him, hoping that common sense would find him, or thank God that Charlene's father didn't have a better swing.

*There was really nothing either one of them could do at this point.*

*"I know someone who can fix this, but you know Grandma will see it before I get a chance," said Deon.*

*"If and when Grandma sees the dent, we'll come up with a story. I don't even have enough energy to tell you what you should and shouldn't have done. The best thing I can tell you to do is to get some rest. Come on," she said, motioning towards the door. She could lie and say Will hit it while backing out if it came down to it. It wouldn't be the first time she had taken the blame for one of Deon's mistakes.*

*He turned back to look at the car one last time before walking into the house. The two parted ways as they went to their rooms and let the night take away their cares. Deon was more than okay with forgetting about it for now. He appeared more shaken up than usual from his latest run in with Charlene's father. If you didn't press his buttons, Mr. Brown was a pretty decent man. He was pretty much a gentle giant to everyone in the neighborhood, but Deon knew which buttons to press with him and did so at every chance that was afforded to him. As Jacquelyn settled back into her bed she could only imagine the new troubles her little brother had borrowed this time. Her thoughts soon settled as sleep finally found her.*

*The following morning Jacquelyn was yet again startled from her sleep by Deon, only this time, he didn't request that she get up he demanded.*

*"Jacquelyn, wake up. Grandma's going outside to get the mail, and you know the first thing she'll see is the car!"*

Jacquelyn didn't even have a chance to wipe the sleep from her eyes.

"Alright, Deon, just be cool. Let the situation handle itself before you go out and tell on yourself." Jacquelyn knew that kids were always playing in front of their yards, so she knew the blame for the car ordeal could easily be shifted to completely pass over Deon. "Listen, let the neighborhood kids be scape goat this time," she said before rolling over. Jacquelyn thought about her previous idea of allowing her beau to shoulder the blame and reconsidered. Lena was actually quite fond of Will and there was no need to sour her feelings towards him because of her baby brother's latest act of negligence. They heard the front door slam shut as they walked towards the kitchen. Uncle Ray was sitting at the kitchen table sipping coffee while Aunt Gwen fried bacon on the stove. The smell of hot coffee and fresh bacon grease was a comforting scent Jacquelyn, but she couldn't even indulge in the aroma. Gwen was the first to speak.

"Well, good morning. It's good to see my niece and nephew in the same room without a frown on your faces and foolishness coming from your mouths," she teased.

"I can say the same to you," responded Jacquelyn, looking towards Uncle Ray. With that said Gwen returned to stirring a pot of grits and looked away from Jacquelyn and Deon. Clearly, the remarks went over Ray's head. He continued reading the paper without hesitation or second thought about what either woman had said. Gwen opened her mouth again to make a snide remark, but all the focus went to Lena as soon as she walked in. Lena walked in, slamming the door behind her. Jacquelyn and Deon studied her face for any kind of emotion. She finally let out a sigh of frustration.

"Mama, where's the mail," asked Gwen.

"One of those kids running the streets must have run into the car with their bike or something. They left a nice-sized dent on the side." Jacquelyn searched Lena's face for a faint crease or brow raise that would indicate she knew the truth. This time even Queen couldn't read her face. While Deon and Jacquelyn were watching Lena's face, Ray had been doing the same to them. Now the two stood motionless, waiting for their grandmother's reaction.

"Well, I didn't hear or see any kids out in the front yard this morning," Gwen had to add her comments to the conversation as usual. Ray spoke up, "You were probably too busy running your mouth. Sometimes these things happen, especially when you got a neighborhood full of kids running around. I'll go check on it later Lena. In the meantime, I'm going to the back to wake my boy up." He cleared his throat, and Jacquelyn and Deon made room for him to pass through.

Lena went about her morning routine as her grandchildren felt basked in temporary relief. The rest of the day went as planned. Deon was busy running the streets, and Jacquelyn felt comfortable with the thought of "out of sight and out of mind" when it came to him, especially today. Lena took her frustrations out through housework. Deon looked on the bright side of things. They might not have had a clean conscience, but at least they'd have a clean house. Jacquelyn was involved with that car more than usual on that day. Out *of all the days she could have used it, she was the chauffeur for everyone else.*

*"Hey, Queen, I need you to take me to work today," said Gwen. "Oh, and your Uncle Ray needs you to carry him to an interview today," she mumbled to herself. "Carry him. Finally, someone else can take the load off my back. Ha! Carry, that's what I've been doing for the past six months." Jacquelyn could still hear her as she left her room, shaking her head in discontent. Jacquelyn knelt at her closet door, looking for her shoes, as she felt two small hands covering her eyes.*

*"Guess who?" asked a small voice. She smiled and played along. Her little cousin Chris was one of her few soft spots.*

*"Hmm...let me guess," she said as she reached behind and grabbed his small frame, tickling him. His squeals of joy would brighten up anyone's mood. His tight coils shook from his laughter as he squirmed on the floor. A moment later Gwen strolled in, breaking up the sweet bonding moment between the two. Standing in the doorway with both hands on her hips, "Queen, we got things to do. Let's get to it." Jacquelyn grabbed a giggly Chris, and they met outside. Uncle Ray was on his knees inspecting the car.*

*"Yep, that's a big dip," said Gwen rubbing her hand against the car. I'm sure that would've made some kind of noise." Jacquelyn spoke up.*

*"Not necessarily. Sometimes these things just happen." She caught herself repeating her Uncle's words. Ray added, "Yeah, one of these kids playing around here. But dent or no dent, it'll get us to where we need to go today, everybody in."*

*Today Jacquelyn was not the only one covering for Deon. Ray effortlessly helped to smooth things over. He would gladly pick up the slack if it meant he heard less noise from his wife's mouth.*

## Chapter 3

*The whole car episode ended quicker than it began. It faded admist the string of episodes Deon dragged Jacquelyn in and out of. She turned the page and flipped to another familiar date. Jacquelyn didn't even get through the last line of the entry before her senses drew her back to the evening before the date Lena had written. She could still hear Donny Hathaway playing as she approached the front door. A chill in the air made Jacquelyn less patient with the stubborn front door. The lock on the door always seemed to jam during cold weather, and this night was no exception. After a slight amount of patience Jacquelyn opened the door and saw the two empty chairs where Gwen and Ray had been seated. One of them had been pushed over. Jacquelyn could already tell that this was not a sign of a heat of the moment romantic gesture. The chill from outside had also invited itself inside their home. What was meant to be a quiet night between them seemed like it had turned into a classic Gwen moment. Jacquelyn wondered how long it had taken her Aunt to ruin it all. Gwen knew how to rattle Ray, and attacking his pride was her favorite trigger. However, judging by the half-eaten chicken on their plates and empty glasses, Gwen might have* taken the slower route this time. Lena and Chris trailed in behind her from down the hallway.

"I know they did not break my favorite vase!" said a stunned Lena. A door slammed, and they heard Ray's baritone voice clearly irritated.

"No. Not tonight! I'm not wearing my back out tonight, at least not on that old couch." The three of them went to the hallway to get a better view of what was going on.

"Well, too bad cause tonight you and the couch are going to be reacquainted." Gwen's loud mouth was not even muffled from behind the other side of the door. Lena walked up to Ray, still staring at the closed door.

"Ray, what happened, honey?" He began to explain when his voice was overshadowed.

"He ruined my joy once again!" answered Gwen.

"See, it's stuff like that," he said, facing Lena. He turned to the door, "I'm not your child. I can answer for myself. Your child is standing in the hall." Ray paused after becoming aware of his son's presence. He walked away from Lena and picked up his son. Holding him close, he told Lena, "I can't do this right now. She just wants to go back and forth. I can't." He walked away, carrying his son to the room he shared with Deon. "I'm sure Deon won't mind if I use his bed tonight," he said before calmly ending his quarrel with his wife. Seeing that he was obviously drained from Gwen's countless attempts to break him down, Lena had had enough of it herself.

"Open the door," she commanded firmly without raising her voice. Gwen obeyed her mother's request. Lena entered the room, and Jacquelyn followed behind her. Gwen hopped over and closed the door. Lena shook her head disapprovingly.

"Closed doors say a lot about a home," said her mother. Jacquelyn sat on the bed as her Aunt and grandmother faced one another. "Every time I turn around, you are cutting that man down. To be such a dignified man, he always holds his tongue for you. I love you, but you know that you have a strong man for him to have stuck with you after everything you have put him through."

Gwen quickly responded, "Maybe if he didn't give me a reason, I wouldn't have to cut him down." "What reason did he give you this time?"

"Mama, everything was going fine. He was looking good. I was looking better," she said, winking toward Jacquelyn before continuing. Gwen hid behind her conceited wit. It was her way of deflecting. "Even the conversation was going great. I hadn't even raised my voice once. Then we got on the subject of his job. I told him how I was proud of him and his progress at the shop, and then the next thing I knew, he talked about getting a loan and starting a car service. I don't..." Lena interrupted her.

"The whole time you've been talking, the one thing that keeps coming out of your mouth is "I." Baby, it's not always about you. Sometimes you have to sacrifice what you want for someone else's happiness." Gwen once again brought the attention back to herself.

"I just don't want to spend my life giving up everything I want just to cater to some man like you." Gwen paused and looked away from her mother. Lena looked at her and tried to speak but simply said,

"I'm done," and threw her hands up as she walked away. Gwen was striking out with everyone that night. She looked over at Jacquelyn, who was now the only one left.

"That's not what I meant. That's not what I meant to say," she said, almost whispering as she walked closer to her niece. Jacquelyn looked at her Aunt, whose entire countenance had changed. Her bold and defiant pose with her hands on her hips had now melted into a modest slump. Gwen sat on the bed, reminding Jacquelyn of Chris when he did something wrong or something didn't go his way. "I know I was wrong," Gwen said, finally breaking the silence. This was a rarity for her Aunt to admit that she was wrong. Humble was word far removed from Gwen, but it was befitting in this moment.

"Why are you so hard on Uncle Ray? I mean, I know it's your business, but it seems like he's really trying. He went from riding in the best cars to working under them. Plus, he has to work with Deon every day. Even I have to give him credit for that," she said, hoping to get a smile out of her Aunt, which Jacquelyn knew wouldn't be easy. She couldn't even get a smirk. Once again, Gwen alleviated Jacquelyn from her loss of words.

"None of this is new. I know where it started, but I never thought it would still be so many more nights like this one. When we lost Miranda, it almost severed our relationship. That's the root of all of the one-sided arguments," said Gwen after several minutes of silence. Jacquelyn was surprised to hear her Aunt's words that seemed to come from nowhere. She hadn't heard anyone mention her cousin's name in years.

Miranda's pictures were scarce throughout her grandmother's home since Gwen said she needed time to heal. Time obviously did not heal all wounds because those pictures had stayed packed away from then on. The collateral damage that came from each loss in the Hart family created little fractures that each member became accustomed to. The gradual rifts had taken its toll on each relationship, but Gwen and Ray's marriage was the most noticeable. On the surface Gwen found it easier to pretend that the burden on her marriage came from the financial burdens and bad business deals that her husband made. The truth is Gwen's vanity held no comparison to her grief. She learned that loss isn't something you just get over. You accept it. Learn to live with it until it becomes a part of you. That part of you that either disguise itself in your everyday smile that you put on to make everyone else comfortable or devours you whole if you lose balance.

"I know that was devastating for the both of you, but I didn't know how deep the damage ran. The two of you seemed okay until Uncle Ray's business deals went downhill." Gwen was taken aback by her niece's bold assumption.

"If you're insinuating that the money made everything okay, you really have no idea who I am as a woman or a mother. Believe me. I'm not as heartless as any of you think. I may be a little shallow, but I'm not heartless. No one knows what losing our daughter really did to us. You know, that day she died, she was supposed to be here with Mama, but she couldn't because Daddy was sick. Ray refused to take a day off because he had some stupid meeting. I couldn't miss another day from my job. I either had to take care of Miranda when she had chicken pox or Ray when he had the flu. All of that added up to me being inches away from a pink slip. I ended up being stuck with Ray's fickle cousin Lisa as my only option. I had a gut feeling that I should've just risked that job instead of leaving my baby with that idiot. I was at my desk for less than two hours when I got that call. It only took me a few minutes to get to Lisa's house. I took one look at my baby's body, and I knew that there was no way the paramedics could bring her back. Lisa had been too busy running her mouth on the phone to notice that Miranda had fallen into the pool. I could have killed Ray's cousin if those officers hadn't been there. By the time Ray got there, our daughter was being carted off in a body bag. I placed a lot of my guilt on him. You think our fighting is bad now? Please! We were ten times worse back then." Jacquelyn remembered her aunt briefly moving in with her grandparents. She didn't have all of the details as she allowed Gwen to fill in the missing pieces.

"Sure, Ray's a good husband and father now. That day will always stay with me, though. I think that piece of me that died was a small part of my love for him."

Jacquelyn picked up where Gwen left off.

"Is that why you waited so long to have Chris? Because you were afraid you would lose another baby?" Gwen shook her head. "No, I wasn't afraid. I just knew how to hold a grudge. I know it wasn't Ray's fault, but I figured since he made me feel like I didn't matter, I would make him feel like it didn't *matter when it came to giving him another child. I know I'm selfish, but I'm working on it."*

*"We're all working on something, I guess," said Jacquelyn after hugging her and walking to the door.*

*Jacquelyn gained a better sense of Gwen. Jacquelyn assumed she shared this part of her life with her because she needed someone to understand her position. At least now, she knew one of the reasons behind her snappy attitude toward Uncle Ray. A couple of days went by before Ray and Gwen spoke. Most of the silence was filled in with a couple of smart comments from her Aunt. Jacquelyn now figured it was a part of her nature. When they finally did speak, Gwen apologized. It must have been the first time since she said "I'm sorry" to him because it seemed enough to end their little feud...for now.*

Chapter 4

*February 12, 1978*

*My house is filled with a bunch of children. Yeah, they may be grown, but they still have plenty of growing up to do. Gwen and Ray get along for a few days and then go right back at it again when they think things have gotten too peaceful. Queen and Deon are getting along better than usual, which means one of them is hiding something from me. The two of them find a way to come together to scheme. The truth will come to light soon.*

*As a parent you pour every bit of yourself into your child and you hope it's more of the good than the bad that takes hold. You hope that one day they see you as human too. Parents aren't perfect, and we really just want our babies to be happy & at peace. Despite the layers of lessons, words of wisdom, arguments and countless prayers you want the simplest of things, happiness. I say a prayer for each of children and grandchildren and an extra one for their guardian angels because Lord knows they keep them busy!*

*Jacquelyn found herself staring in the mirror on that same day. She was stuck deciding on whether to intervene between her brother and his new friend. She had seen him the night before when she was out with Charlene. She was "cute as a button," Lena would say. Although short, her stature certainly did not fit her attitude, especially once she met her boiling point, much like her father. She had grown up with the biggest childhood crush on Deon, and when he finally took notice, poor Charlene didn't stand a chance. Her naïve and childlike trust made her a prime target for Deon to manipulate. She loved her brother, but even she wouldn't dismiss his behavior towards Charlene. No amount of girl chats could push Charlene away. Everyone knew heartbreak was inevitable, yet that would be the only way for things to end the pair.*

*Will had canceled on Jacquelyn, and Deon told Charlene that they "need to do their own thing apart." As children Jacquelyn and Charlene had spent more time together before boys called themselves "discovered" them, aka when hormones became the dictators of their relationships. When the two ladies were younger they would spend the entire day watching movies at Ralph's Cinema making countless trips to fill up on popcorn and soda. Afterwards they would dissect each film like movie critics. Jacquelyn loved the thrillers. Charlene would cover her eyes on every gory scene while digging her nails into Jacquelyn bare arm. Of course, being the hopeless romantic Charlene's picks were always filled with great love affairs and whimsical fairytale endings. They met in the middle with comedies. Charlene had the quirkiest laugh that Jacquelyn lived for whenever they saw any silly movies. Even if the scene lacked in hilarity, her friend's laughter made up for it.*

*Right before they entered the movie theater, Charlene caught sight of Deon down the street at the corner store. She had to squint her eyes to see if she was correct.*

*"Isn't that your brother over there," she said pointing. Before Jacquelyn had a chance to answer, Charlene was yelling his name. "Deon...Deon, you know you hear me!"*

*Jacquelyn looked in the young man's direction to see if it was him. Charlene continued calling after him, but he paid her no mind and looked around as if he did not want to be seen. The person Deon was talking to didn't seem to be bothered by any of his unwanted attention. He was not very tall, but his muscular frame managed to give him an intimidating frame. He seemed much older than Deon and did not look like any of his usual friends or associates that Jacquelyn could remember. She interrupted Charlene's failed attempt to catch his eye.*

*"Maybe it's not him. You know he would have been over here the first time you called. Anyway, you know they say everyone has a twin somewhere. I think that's how it goes," she said, smiling. Her friend was not buying into her idea. "Let's just enjoy our movie." Charlene did not want to argue, though. She tried to save all of her harsh words for Deon. She smiled a little to appease her friend and followed her to the theater.*

*Now Jacquelyn stood in the bathroom in front of the mirror, waiting to hear a bang from the other side of the door. Usually, Deon would be banging on the door, trying to rush* his sister or whomever out of the bathroom by now. Instead, all she heard, besides the regular morning noise between everyone else in the house, was the dripping sink. Evidently, her brother wanted to avoid answering questions about the previous day. Lately Deon seemed so mysterious, and more like a visitor in their home. He crept in late that previous night before just to avoid his sister. She tried to shake off her misgivings of her brother and how he spent his time. Jacquelyn knew her brother and knew something was wrong whenever he tried to stay out of her sight. Her concern for him hovered over her throughout the entire day. It even interrupted her date with Will. He tried to ease her mind the best that he could. Jacquelyn explained her apprehensions to Will regarding Deon. Will admired their close bond, but advised her that her constant need to baby her brother would only stunt his growth.

"I know that's your brother, but he's not a five-year-old that has to run to you every time he needs help."

"Help? That usually means there's a problem. Do you think something's wrong?" she asked.

"Stop being so paranoid. Let him be a man. If he had a problem, he would come to you. Like always, he added.

"The problem is he's not a man. And what was that comment supposed to mean?" asked Jacquelyn as she pushed her plate *away. Her appetite had quickly faded. The discussion would turn into a debate, and an argument would ensue.*

*He quickly responded.*

*"It means that it's time for you to stop being so caught up in his life and catch up on your own," he said while pushing her plate back across the table to her.*

*"Can we please get back to us?" he asked as he reached for her hand. She nodded and returned his smile. She knew what Will was saying was true. She just had to find her own way to let go. Jacquelyn saw herself as her brother's safe haven, allowing him to walk into manhood was going to be easier said than done.*

*By the time Will took her home, Jacquelyn had expected to walk into the house with everyone asleep except for Lena because her grandmother had to have her late-night tea. She also expected to see her aunt and uncle getting into their last little disagreement of the day. Yet, she saw that Lena was the only one that stuck to her routine. Gwen and Ray were cuddled on the love seat with Chris nestled against Ray, very uncommon, but welcome scene for Jacquelyn to witness. Lena came in from the kitchen, sipping on her cup of mint tea.*

*On the way home they saw the luminous sign for Collin's Skating Rink beaming at the red light. A mischievous grin came across Will's face as they both glanced in the direction. Jacquelyn glanced over and broke out in laughter. "I can read your mind William Jacobs. Nope! We are not repeating history."*

*"Come on now. For old time's sake let's take spin down memory lane. I promise I won't let you fall...this time."*

*"It was more like a stumble than a spin for me." Collin's Skating Rink was where they had their first date. Will had insisted on meeting there after Jacquelyn told one little white lie of how good of skater she was. Truthfully Jacquelyn had two left feet on the dancefloor which translated right over to her being a horrible skater. Wanting to impress him she agreed to go to the rink. Jacquelyn's friends Avery and Doris gave her their best on the fly lessons. Doris made it look so natural as she skated backwards twirling around in the cul-de-sac. Betty tried to help balance a wobbly Jacquelyn. Despite the girls' best efforts they knew Jacquelyn's derriere would spend more time on the skate floor than all eight of her wheels. After a grueling seven hours of practice which consisted of countless falls, scrapes and half a box of Band-Aids, Jacquelyn figured she was ready as she's ever be for her date with Will. Thankfully she wore bellbottoms to cover her bandaged knees. She remembered holding her breath then repeating balance, balance, balance, a mantra she developed from her hurried lessons. Her memory of arriving to the skating rink was blurred due to her nerves being a wreck. This could down in history as being the most embarrassing night of her teenage life. She envisioned herself gliding gracefully while she waited as Will grabbed her skates, and envisioned her. Will plopped beside her with the heavy footwear. "The new skates go fast, but I made sure*

*they tightened each wheel. You wouldn't believe how many accidents I've seen even with skilled skaters like yourself."*

*Jacquelyn let out a nervous giggle. She took her time lacing mini death traps attached to her feet. She stood up surprisingly well without a single wobble. "Let's glide," she said motioning towards the busy floor. With each step she grew slightly more confident. Now was the real test as they stepped onto the freshly polished wooden floor. Will held Jacquelyn's hand as they followed the crowd. To her delight Will teetered a bit when one of the faster patrons zoomed past them. Maybe he'll fall first, bruise his ego and I'll let him off the hook by saying we can leave early. No need for further embarrassment. Unfortunately for her Will gained his footing and began skating backwards. She repeated, "Balance, balance, balance..." under her breath as "Hollywood Swingers" blared over the speakers. The seasoned skaters zoomed around her. Jacquelyn increased her speed and even started to enjoy her stride. She saw Will spin around her narrowly throwing her off of her balance. "Uh, are your skates comfortable?" he asked puzzled. "Sure. Why do you ask?"*

*"No offence, but you look like your feet hurt. They might have given you the wrong size." She laughed anxiously, "Now that you mention it they do feel a little snug. He grabbed her hand guiding her at a swifter pace. "No worries. We can switch them out." When they were halfway around near the exit a kid no more than nine pushed past the two, breaking their interlocked fingers and completely ruining Jacquelyn's ruse. Will was able to rebound quickly, but Jacquelyn wasn't as lucky. By the time Will turned around Jacquelyn was in*

midair. She realized balance had betrayed her and was completely missing. She flapped around like a baby bird getting kick out of its nest. Her next sights were of her feet in the air and the ceiling. Her pride and her rear end were sorely bruised. Will swooped in and gathered her from the floor revealing her jeans that had completely split down the middle. He took her out for ice cream on their second date. Jacquelyn was left with a twisted ankle and a promise from Will to never take her back to Collin's Rink.

Back to the present moment, she declined his invitation to revisit the ego crushing premises. "I preferred our second date. A banana split pronto. It's befitting." She repeated what he said when he ordered it way back then. She didn't appreciate the joke at the time. "What the Queen wants the Queen gets." He shrugged laughing at the memory of Jacquelyn's misfortune.

"Hey, Queen. Early night," said Lena, while glancing at the clock.

"Yes, but it was nice. No fussing, well not too much," she said smiling, closing the door behind her.

"I know. I'm just teasing you. All of my babies seem to be getting along right now. It's a nice surprise to see those two in the same room without each other on the opposite end, about to break the noise barrier. What's going on with you and your brother, though?" she asked, quickly shifting the focus of the conversation.

"Nice transition," said Jacquelyn. She did not know how to answer the question because she did not know where she and her brother stood at the moment. "I haven't gotten a chance to figure that out myself. For the past couple of days, when he's at one place, I'm at another. I don't know. I kind of think he's running away from me. When I find out, you'll be the first to know," she said, anticipating her grandmother's response. "Is he here?" asked Jacquelyn.

"No. He came in and went back a little while after you left. I know he's not with Charlene because she stopped by a little earlier, but he wouldn't go to the door. That poor girl really loves him. Anyway, after that, he rode off in a gray car with one of his friends... I guess."

"You guess? I'm surprised you didn't follow him," she said, teasing Lena.

"Well, I was tempted, but I figured it would be best if I stayed out of his business." Jacquelyn quickly commented.

"I guess that makes two of us. Will and I were just talking about that tonight." Her grandmother smiled at the mention of Will's name. Lena loved him. In her words, he was a consistent man in such an unpredictable world. As she told Jacquelyn, this was a rare but valuable find in anyone, especially a potential husband. Her grandmother anxiously awaited the day her Queen would come home with an engagement ring from Will. She even had a bottle of champagne reserved for that particular day. She had

Jacquelyn follow her to the kitchen table to sit down and chat without disturbing the others.

"Now, tell me all about Will." She studied her granddaughter's face. "And I want to know the truth." Jacquelyn began,

"I know he cares and everything, but it seems like his biggest concern is fitting into this mold that his father's company has made for him." Lena looked at her, puzzled.

"What's wrong with having a set plan? He's thinking about the future."

"Nothing's wrong with that, but I'm thinking about the future also. And I don't want to b**-e married to someone more devoted to some image than his family." Lena quickly interrupted,

"Married. Does that mean ..." Her excitement was short-lived.

"No, no, not quite yet. His father is grooming him to become his partner for the magazine. Sometimes that's all he can talk about, and I find myself just sitting there nodding my head, saying, "Yeah, uh huh." Then I just wonder where I fit into the conversation. I mean, we do talk about other stuff, but..." She paused, pulling her words back into place. "I don't want to sound ungrateful because I know he does care; sometimes, I don't think I fit into his perfect world."

"Why? You don't feel like you belong because of money? Did those uppity people around him say anything to you? You

know I don't have a problem with calling them up."
Jacquelyn laughed, amused by her,

"No, Grandma."

"No to what?" asked Lena.

"No to everything. I'm secure with myself anyway. I just wish he could push more of his focus towards me and creating his own path. I didn't know relationships were this much work." Lena smiled, shaking her head.

"Well, if you love him, you can make it work."

"Grandma, that doesn't solve my problem. You can't stick the word love on a bruise and hope it'll get better."

"I'm not saying that Queen, but you learn how to sacrifice for one another. Take the time to think about a solution. It worked for me." Jacquelyn didn't feel like spending the rest of her night going back and forth with Lena, so she nodded and said okay. "Oh, baby, before you go to your room, can you carry Chris to his bed? I want to keep this picture of the two of them at peace for as long as I can," Lena said, pointing towards Gwen and Ray. Jacquelyn quietly walked over to the couch and cradled him in her arms. Lena walked over to where her grandchildren were, kissing them both.

"Goodnight, my babies," she whispered.

Jacquelyn placed Chris into his bed and tried to put her concerns about Deon and Will to rest.

The next day came and slowly drifted by while she worked at the boutique. The owner, Angela, had just about handed the operation over to Queen. It was Jacquelyn's place in every way except for the deed. Hopefully, that would belong to her soon as well. Angela had been toying with the idea of selling the boutique. Jacquelyn's problem was coming up with the funds. Her day almost slipped away when the door chime welcomed a familiar customer. She turned around to see Deon.

"Hey stranger," she said with one hand firmly on her hip and the other grasping roses. He just snickered at her remark.

"Where have you been, and why have you been tip-toeing around me?"

"Nobody's tip-toeing around you, and I'm here now, so it doesn't matter. Anyway, I'm a grown man, so where I was shouldn't be your concern." She rolled her eyes, saying,

"Yeah, okay. You'll be a grown man when you don't have to remind me and everyone else by repeating it over and over again."

"Yeah, yeah. Can I just stop by to see my big sister without hearing the extra mess?"

"Mmhmm. I know you, though. And why do you look like a delivery boy with all those flowers?

"I need to drop off a few bundles for a few special ladies. I thought I'd start with you, and before you get a million crazy thoughts in your head, they're for Grandma, Gwen, and Charlene." He smiled and handed her the yellow roses. He left just as Angela was walking in. She said hello and winked as *he held the door open for her.*

*"Always the gentleman," Angela said to Deon as he departed.*

*"Girl, if I was about fifth-teen years younger, well, let's say I'd be a part of the family by now," Angela said partially jokingly.*

*"Yeah, whatever you say, Angie." Jacquelyn thought to herself, "That boy is slicker than I thought. He managed to completely get away from the subject of him avoiding me."*

*"I guess I didn't come out empty-handed," she said aloud, looking down at her flowers. She didn't even pay Angela's remarks any attention.*

*Oh well, I'll get my chance to talk to him later on tonight. I have to give him credit for the flowers, she thought. Yet, even with the facade that her brother had put on, Jacquelyn could not get past the frustration of not knowing what was going on with him. With the boutique only being a few blocks away that gave her very little time to think things through on her walk back home. She arrived just as Ray was pulling into the driveway. He swung open the car door and noticed her flowers.*

*"Roses. Uh-oh, did Will do something wrong or just a special occasion?"*

*"Neither. They're from Deon. I guess he decided I was special today, but I'm more interested in finding out the reason behind your smile." Gwen had finally given Ray her blessing to start his limousine service. Now all he needed to move forward with his plan was financial backing.*

*"Well," he paused for a second. "You know I hate repeating myself, so let's share the good news with everyone." They*

*walked through the door together. Chris ran straight to Ray with a sticky grape jelly face and peanut butter fingers to match. Gwen came around the corner chasing behind him.*

*"Boy, come here! You're about to get that mess all on your Daddy." He had marked her two minutes before Jacquelyn and Ray walked through the door. There was a large smudge of jelly on her left thigh. Ray picked him up anyway, saying,*

*"Never mind that I've been dirty before." She placed her hands on her chest, presumably tired from chasing him around. "Baby, you look beautiful today," said Ray. She looked at herself suspiciously after his compliment. Besides her noticeable peanut butter stain, she wore her old faded jeans with a jelly-stained blouse. In her words, "This is not a good look." Instead of dismissing his compliment, she said,*

*"Okay, Deon gave me flowers today. I mean, the boy is nice but not that nice. Now you're telling me how good I look. Yes, I know I look good, but even the best can't pull this look off. I knew bad news was gonna follow it. What's wrong?" He stopped her before her suspicions escalated.*

*"Nothing's wrong," he assured her. "Where's your Mama and Deon? I want the whole family to hear me."*

*"Mama is in the kitchen, and Deon is with Charlene. They found Lena in the kitchen, where Gwen approached her first.*

*"Everyone knows I've been waiting to hear from the bank about the loan. Well, I got the news today. I didn't get the loan." Gwen's face dropped, and her eyebrows lifted as if to say what are you so happy about? Ray went on, "But I got a call from my cousin. I told him about my idea before I even*

applied for the loan. Remember when he and his wife were going through that rough patch, and she kicked him out, then I gave him the money to get a place to stay?" he said, looking towards his wife.

"Yeah, and we fought about it for two weeks," she answered.

"He remembers it too. He's giving me the money."

Gwen ran to him, hugging him the way Chris would, full of childlike excitement.

"Oh, thank you, Jesus!" was Lena's response.

"He said I need to pick a building, and he'll fly down here with the check before the ink dries. He called it a little seed money." Gwen headed out of the kitchen. "Where are you going?" He asked.

"I need to change. We're finding a building today."

He laughed at her excitement. Gwen appreciated her mother's hospitality but loved having her place again more than staying in the house she'd left behind so many times before. Within a few weeks Ray's plan went from wishful thinking to full operation. He wasted no time bringing his dream into fruition with the investment from his cousin Doris. Ray utilized all of his resources from former classmates, coworkers, to a few of Lena and Franks connections to build his clientele for his luxury limousine service. The new success of that came with Ray's Luxury Fleet ignited a flame that garnered attention on the Hart family. It also sparked a flame in Ray's life that had dimmed when he initially returned back to his home town. Returning back to one's roots can illicit feelings of either triumph or defeat. Both Ray and Gwen felt nothing more than defeat with their return. With the fledgling business making waves the two were now brimming over with hope for their family's future. Their ascending reputation created a ripple affect Lena couldn't help but take note of.

A new morning brought about the same routine for Jacquelyn. She found herself repeating the same habits as her mother. She applied the lotion first and a splash of her favorite perfume last. As a child her mother's scent was one of the last things to fade from her memory. When Jacquelyn would disappear in the house, Lena knew exactly where to find her, tucked away in the back room clutching her mother's Sunday coat. The coat held the lingering fragrance that comforted little Jacquelyn the way condolences never could. Lena had managed to track down a bottle of the elusive fragrance for her granddaughter's fourteenth birthday. Jacquelyn remembered the moment she opened the bottle and inhaled deeply. Tears welled in her eyes as she felt like she had gained a tiny piece of her mother back. The familiarity of the perfume granted her forgotten moments with her mother, moments that she clung to even on her darkest days. She parted her hair down the middle, and smiled at her reflection as it reminded her of her mother. Deon came into her room right in the middle of her routine.

"Morning Queen."

"Hey." She responded without looking up from applying her lipstick. Deon looked at her roses, sitting in a water-filled vase beside the window. "At least somebody appreciates my effort," he said, leaning against the dresser. Jacquelyn could sense the pout on his face before peering up at her brother. She knew instinctively that he was there for a bruised ego and consoling from his big sister. With the distance that he had created recently, Jacquelyn was actually happy to oblige.

"Who upset my big baby?" she teased.

"I don't understand you women. One day you're calling a man non-stop, and the next day when he shows you some attention, you're throwing his flowers back at him. Then while you ignore him, he's left pulling thorns and pedals from his face."

"So, I'm guessing Charlene didn't care for those special roses you gave her? You really can't expect too much. You ignored the girl when she was yelling your name the other day, and don't act like it wasn't you," she said, pointing at him.

"You can't be all over a person one minute, and then completely give them the cold shoulder the next."

Jacquelyn had a low tolerance for Deon treating Charlene as he did. She was not just his girlfriend; she was also her friend and would remain so before and after the demise of their relationship. Jacquelyn did not like to think so negatively about their relationship, but at the rate Deon was going, it was inevitable. When it came to maturity Deon had stalled and there were no signs of him growing up any time soon. As much as she hated to admit, Jacquelyn knew she was part of the problem. Jacquelyn could hear previous conversations with Will echoing in her ears. He constantly reminded her of her hand in Deon's immaturity each time she made the mistake of vent to him about her brother. That was an entirely different issue she'd have to address, but at this *point, she could only be honest with him regarding his relationship woes.*

*"I know you have a five-second attention span, but Charlene needs way more time than what you've been giving her. And a quick stroll to the corner store and back does not count as quality time. What no quick come back at me?"*

*Usually, by this time, Deon would have interrupted her before she finished her first sentence. Although he always asked for her opinion, he wanted her to tell him what he wanted to hear, like most people. He allowed Jacquelyn's words to sink in.*

*"The last thing I need is another issue with her, especially now," Deon muttered.*

*Jacquelyn raised her eyebrow and looked at him perplexed. She wondered what was so important about "right now". The two had plenty of snags in the past, so why was the present such lousy timing? He answered his sister as if he were reading her expression.*

*"It's nothing too big," he said, trying to brush it off. "I'm thinking about moving to California with Charlene," he blurted out. She wasted no time responding.*

*"Nothing too big?" She said while hitting him with her brush.*

*"Jacquelyn, stop. Okay, you only get one more strike before I pick up the comb on you! Hitting me won't change my mind." He let go of her wrist as she caught her breath.*

*"Yeah, but maybe it'll knock some sense into you. What's made California so important to you?" He sat on the bed beside her.*

*"Charlene's been talking to one of her aunts out there, and she was able to contact her mother a few months ago. You know she's been desperate to find her mother since she left. I can't let her go on her own."*

*Charlene's childhood obsession was the mother that had been pushed out of her life. Mr. Brown tried wiping Mrs. Brown's memory from his daughter's mind. He took away every photo his wife was in, threw away all her clothes, and banned her relatives from speaking to Charlene. His child became just another possession of his wife that couldn't be disposed of. As she grew and her mother's features blossomed through her, the more his resentment strangled their relationship. Mrs. Brown's departure had created such a scandal at the time. So much of the gossip and awkward stares that followed him could be blamed for his bitter spirit towards the neighbors. The Browns were once the perfect family that so many* envied. Yet, perfection's flaws were exposed when Mrs. Brown's affair was discovered. The anger that Mr. Brown felt took over and seeped through his body, almost causing him to destroy his wife with his bare hands, but instead, he took another route. A formal goodbye between mother and daughter was not even granted. In his opinion, his wife was lucky to be leaving with her life. For years Charlene was led to believe that her mother had run out on her. That feeling of abandonment lived in every relationship that she made.

"This is what she needs, and this isn't your issue. I'm not a little kid. I can handle this. I will handle this. I'll still take care of my family." A stunned Jacquelyn spoke after a few seconds.

"Wow. I can only imagine what her father has to say about this."

"He doesn't know, and until we make it to California, it has to stay that way. He hated her mother back then, and he hates me now. If he knew, he'd cut Charlene off from the few people she has left." Jacquelyn agreed.

"Okay. You know he won't hear anything from me, but just think about who you're going against. He's crazy, and anyone around here can attest to that. If I had a chance to see our mama even one more time, I know I'd take it in a heartbeat. I wouldn't let anything stop me, either. I can't blame her. Everything else probably doesn't even matter to her anymore. So, what's your plan when you do get there?" asked Jacquelyn.

"Hopefully, Charlene gets to see her mom. We'll put the details together later. I don't need you to sort this out for me, *but I need you to be there for us. Can you do that without taking over?"* Deon asked hoping for his sister's reassurance.

*They sat there for a moment, neither one of them speaking. Jacquelyn's curiosity got the best of her. "So, how long will you two be gone? Maybe a couple of days, weeks, months?" The more she went on, the more nervous she became. Her brother's prolonged response increased her fears.*

*"We haven't gotten to that part yet. We're still working things out with her aunt. Charlene hasn't even had a chance to speak to her mama," said Deon.*

## Chapter 5

*April 27, 1978 The family is changing and drifting in day by day. Everyone is walking on a fine line with one another. I've never known any of them to tiptoe around another person's feelings. I don't want them at each other's throats, but something just isn't right. I miss the honest way they used to deal with each other. They put on a front to please me, but I'm not pleased with any of the charades they put on. I'd much rather have them be Frank with me. They may think of me as fragile as far as feelings are concerned, but I've had to deal with plenty of heartaches in my life. My heart is much stronger than they think. If someone doesn't get the truth out soon, I'll do it myself. In the meantime, I'll go along with keeping the peace.*

*Lena's family thought that the less she knew, the happier she would be. However, as the matriarch of the family she took pride in being the liaison amongst the discord. Balancing the scale and ushering in peace was her prime role in the Hart family. Something had recently shifted and now instead of allowing Lena to alleviate their problems, they just let them pile up. As Jacquelyn tried to handle her own issues, she tried even harder to avoid everyone else's dilemmas. It was eating her up, trying to control everything by herself. She felt that now that she was an adult, she should not have to run to her grandmother each time a little stress occurred. Change was like a rapid current in her world, and she was in danger of being carried away. She remembered what her grandmother would always say whenever she faced a problem. "Sink or swim, baby, sink or swim." Jacquelyn was so tired of swimming that sinking did not look too bad. However, each time she felt this way, her family acted as her lifesaver. Who would be the one to pull her to safety while almost every family member was entangled in their own lives? To her surprise, she would reluctantly allow someone else to play the hero.*

## Chapter 6

*Transition. It was the word of the day for Jacquelyn. Her boss Angela had used it with her first when she called her early that morning. She knew this call was unusual because it was unlike Angela to ever call her for any extra help. Angela was so territorial over the boutique. From the ceiling leak that she always said she would fix, but never did to the occasional break in, that had now become less occasional and more on the common side. Angela joked after the most recent break in, "Maybe I should just leave the door unlocked at this point and a thank you note for not busting my glass door. At least they wait until we leave before they make an appearance!" Still Angela prided herself with being one of the longest running businesses on the block and vowed to stay until her twilight years. Jacquelyn knew by her tone that something was off. Jacquelyn twirled the phone cord around with her fingers anticipating whatever she had to tell her.*

*"Jacquelyn, you know that you have been such a great employee. You've become more like a daughter to me. You started out just run errands for me when you were in school, and then you came in full time and you were the best addition to my shop. Sweetie I want you to know I'm really grateful for your hard work over the years. Well, you know, Mr. Huff has been trying to get me to sell my place to him for the past year, and each time he asks, I say no. I was kind of hoping that one day you'd be able to take over from me, but with my mother's health issues and her being so far away..." Angela sighed. Just say it, thought Jacquelyn. She could see*

*the pink slip flying right at her. "I decided to take him up on his offer. I couldn't afford to say no anymore. I'm selling the boutique and my house and moving mother with me to Miami," she said nervously, giggling. "You understand don't you sweetie?"*

*"I do. Angie you know I'll miss you and the shop, but family first" said Jacquelyn. Her heart sank as the words stumbled out of her mouth.*

*"But don't worry because I've already spoken to Mr. Huff, and he's agreed to keep you as an employee when the boutique transition. That's only if you want to stay." Angela, who was usually bubbling over with conversation, on this occasion, she didn't know how to fill in the blank pause that was left.*

*"So, will the shop remain the same after the transition?"*

*"Oh, I think it will be a bar or café, something along those lines."*

*What a way to end it, she thought. Angela had repeatedly said she would never get rid of her boutique because it had such sentimental value. Jacquelyn understood the need to prioritize family, but she also knew Angela was never the "family first" type. Angie had missed countless family occasions because she was always too busy. Jacquelyn knew Angie was conveniently busy because she hated being the baggage that came with the special gatherings. If Angela wasn't being hounded by her nephews for money she was being accosted by her mother about not being married at her age. Her business was her baby, which she proudly proclaimed to Jacquelyn and her loyal patrons.*

*Angela was a talented seamstress and for decades she had made a name for herself designing dresses for the wives of local politicians, church first ladies and even bridal gowns for a few of the founding families.*

*Mr. Huff had proven that his persistence was stronger than any loyalty to the block once dominated by owned establishments. More than half of the block was now owned by Mr. Huff and his investment company. He picked off each business one by one, always going after the establishments with older owners. When Mr. Huff crossed the boutique's threshold Angela immediately knew her place was next on his list. Anytime he'd step foot inside Angela greeted him with, "Buy something pretty for your wife or go." Angela swore her place would never be another casualty. She gossiped about the other store owners who jumped on a deal while handing their companies over.*

*The phone call ended shortly after a few breaks in the conversation, and Jacquelyn was left with more questions for herself. She had not planned on being there forever. She only planned to stay there for a few months after her sophomore year in college. Her grandfather had suffered a stroke and Jacquelyn felt so guilty for not being there. Jacquelyn came back home to help, even though Lena begged her to finish school. Queen's extended break had turned into two years of figuring out what she wanted to do with herself. While she was away at school Jacquelyn found herself spiraling. From endless reports and her streak of swapping majors diminished her excitement of college life she struggled to find her footing. The idea of choosing accounting bored her beyond belief and the thought of becoming a nurse only lasted a moment when she remember the sight of blood turned her legs to Jell-O. She had settled into life using Angie's boutique and her grandmother's home as her safe haven. The truth for Jacquelyn was the idea of leaving family to start a new career and a new life after college scared her more than anything else.*

*"How did I get stuck?" she asked out loud. She now realized that her brief pause somehow became a trap.*

*While everyone was sleeping, the day's worries trickled down to her night. Although Jacquelyn loved the comfort of her grandmother's home, she often wondered, how am I going to get out of this house? Or Should I go back to school? She found that her biggest worries were her indecisiveness and spending the rest of her life trying to escape the dead end she felt she was living. All of her worries could not be solved within one sitting.*

*A visit from Will momentarily distracted her from her thoughts. He convinced her to spend the afternoon with him at the park. With Chris along for the outing, Jacquelyn tried her best to soften her mood. She and Will watched him playing on the playground from a bench a few feet away. He used this as a chance to break through her wall. His simple question of "How are you?" gave him more than he expected.*

*"I just feel like I'm in a hole. I'm the only one stuck while everyone else is moving on. I mean, when I hear good news from someone else, I am happy, genuinely happy for them. But in a way, it's like a blow to the chest. I'm left thinking, damn! When will it be my turn? I know I sound like a big*

kid...so what. That's how I feel. I've gotten used to hearing, "Just be patient" or "It's all in God's timing." I think the most pitiful of them is "keep hope alive." They can keep hope just hand me the dollars and a real chance." He studied her face as if to say, are you done yet? "Oh, you wanted the short version of that. You look like you have something to say." Jacquelyn studied Will's face waiting for a response.

"I didn't want to interrupt you, but now is the best time, given your circumstances. I know you used to love taking pictures. I even remember that one of your majors in college before your hiatus was journalism. That used to be a passion of yours. I have an opening. I want you to be the newest addition to Jacobs Publishing."

"How can my hobby fall into place with a full-time career with your company? I know your father is passing the company down to you, but how do you think he'll react to you hiring someone less seasoned than his other colleagues? And exactly what position is it?"

"Aren't you full of questions for someone who needs a job? As far as my father is concerned, he fully trusts my judgment. Plus, I trust your judgment. Any more questions?"

"What about credentials?" she asked.

"You were on your high school's newspaper for two years, and I know you take your work very seriously. I know your job at Angie's was not what you dreamed of for yourself." Jacquelyn shook her head and scoffed, "With those amazing credentials of course how could I not be a prize candidate?"

Is it that easy? One minute I'm out of a job; the next, he picks up where Angie left off and makes everything all the better *for me? I guess it's all in who you know. Normally I'd be stubborn and give a flat-out no, but I think it deserves some consideration, and my bank account agrees. She didn't question him or his sincerity any further. On a day like this, she accepted what she was given. "I'll consider it. If I didn't know any better, I'd think you were trying to use this as a chance to get closer to me," she said with a wink.*

*"Now, if I didn't know any better, I'd think I was having this conversation with Gwen. I can't be Ray, though, 'cause a man can only take so much no disrespect to your aunt" he said jokingly.*

*"Please, the only thing she and I have in common is the family's good genes."*

*"Now you really sound like her. I think it was the first wink that did it." He watched her as she laughed. "Finally, a real smile on your face, and not the one you give just to be polite. You know, the one you do when you barely show your teeth so they'll get out of your face."*

*"It feels good to get out. Thanks for convincing me to come. Honestly, I thought Chris would be enjoying this more than me." She diverted from the conversation to catch a glance at her cousin. "Hey, wasn't Chris just playing on the monkey bars? I...I just saw him," she said, rising from the bench. "Chris. Chris," she said, almost screaming his name. Jacquelyn did not know what to do first. She had never been placed in a situation like this. She had observed mothers in the market who had lost their children. They would get caught up in whatever item they needed. As soon as they noticed the child's absence, they would go from calmly calling the child to shrieking and running back and forth*

*down the aisle until they bumped into a clerk, blurting out their issue. When they finally united, the mother had more tears in her eyes than the child. Jacquelyn would always think to herself how irresponsible the mother was. Now she felt a rush of guilt.*

*"Chris!" She and Will called for him in unison.*

*"Chris...He couldn't have gone too far. Just stay calm," said Will trying to keep Jacquelyn from sprinting around the park. He held her hand firmly as they quickly moved from each playground section.*

*"Ice cream truck."*

*"What?" asked Jacquelyn blinking back hot tears from her eyes.*

*"I think that's him by the ice cream truck." Sure enough, it was Chris. They made their way to him, and Jacquelyn slowly felt her heart regain its steady beat. She quickly swept him into her arms, almost knocking his ice cream cone out of his fingers.*

*"Don't ever do that again, okay?" Jacquelyn said, looking into his eyes. Her panic slowly lulled, but her body still felt the effects as her legs shook while she struggled to stand still. He shook his head, agreeing as a sticky flow of vanilla ice cream trickled down from the edge of the cone onto his now carefree cousin.*

*"Who got you the cone?" asked Will.*

*"Him," Chris pointed to a face that was not too unfamiliar to Jacquelyn. They had not noticed the man before because of*

*the relief of finding her cousin. The stranger stepped forward.*

*"Hi, I'm an associate of Ray's. I recognized the little guy and assumed he was with his father. I see him from time to time with his mother at the office." He was the same mystery friend Deon was tight-lipped about when she or Charlene brought him up.*

*"Oh, thank you." He must have seen the tension because he cut the one-sided conversation short.*

*"Well, I'll see you around," said the stranger as he waved bye to Chris.*

*"Are you okay?" asked Will. She nodded her head tentatively.*

*"I've seen him before, and it wasn't at Uncle Ray's office. That was just odd, but to answer your question, yeah, I'm much better." She held her cousin close. The side of his face was pressed against hers, warming his cheek from the chill in the air.*

*After Chris's disappearing act, they decided to end their outing and return home. As Will's car pulled into the driveway, he persisted in winning her over as an employee.*

*"Since we're having lunch tomorrow, maybe we can talk about my offer? I don't want to keep you out any later. The street lights are already on, and I don't need Lena coming after me."*

*"I don't think she would give us too much trouble. We both know how she feels about you." Will opened the door for her*

and then carried Chris inside. He'd unsurprisingly fallen asleep during the drive home.

"He had a fun day, to say the least. Plan on telling your Aunt about our unexpected game of hide-n-seek?"

"I think we'll keep this between the three of us." She looked at Chris, sleeping in Will's arms. "If he was awake, I'd get you to pinky swear." Will leaned over to kiss Jacquelyn.

"I think that'll work. Good night."

"Good night." He made sure that she made it into the house before driving away. She put her cousin to bed and later learned that Gwen and Ray had taken this break to have a date night. Lena had made tea for herself and her granddaughter. Lena listened as Jacquelyn told her about her day in between each sip.

"Queen, this really sounds like it would be a good opportunity for you. Plus, it comes with some very nice benefits."

"Grandma, I haven't even found out what the job includes. What benefits could you think of so soon?" Lena raised her eyebrow and lowered her cup enough for Jacquelyn to read her expression. "Oh, I see. You're thinking about getting me down that aisle one way or another. You think that by us working together it'll push us towards the church quicker.

*Nope. We're professionals and will keep it strictly professional in the office. We can do that, right?"*

*"You said the office, but what about outside of the office?" asked Lena smiling.*

*"See, stop that. We can maintain a business relationship."*

*"Does that mean you're accepting his offer?"*

*"Maybe."*

*"Honey, I don't think it's a big deal. You need a job. It's something you enjoy with someone you enjoy being with. If you can't decide, pray about it. Now I'm going to get some rest. Don't stay up too late," she said, kissing Queen on her cheek as she walked by.*

*Jacquelyn remained at the table. She listened to the old house. She had gotten accustomed to the creaks and cracking sounds that it made. When she and her brother first moved in with their grandparents, it took her a while to get used to the periodic snapping of wood. "The house is just settling," her grandfather would say. "There's no need to be afraid. Every old house does it." Jacquelyn thought to herself maybe I'm just settling into my life. Things may snap occasionally, but nothing to be afraid of.*

*"Maybe I am giving this job thing too much thought," she said aloud.*

*"You give everything too much thought, crazy girl. I see you're enjoying another conversation with yourself," said Deon.*

*"I didn't even hear you come in through the door," she said, turning around. "You know me, light on my feet. I lost my key*

*again. I came through my window." She rolled her eyes at her brother's response.*

*"What's with the rip in your pants?" she said, spotting a large tear in the lower half of Deon's slacks. "Rough night with Charlene? I guess she showed you who the boss is."*

*"Yeah, something like that," he said, shrugging off her comment. "You notice everything."*

*"That's a part of my job. Another part of my job is to keep an eye on who my baby brother associates with. I saw your friend again at the park. The one you're so secretive about."*

*"Who? Fred?"*

*"Oh, I finally learn his name. Well, yes, I saw Fred. How did you and Fred become such good friends? He's almost old enough to be our father."*

*"He's a client of Uncle Ray's, and he's not that old. Sometimes I'm his driver. It can be a long ride, so occasionally; I strike up a conversation with the passengers."*

*"Wrong answer. You knew him before you started driving for Uncle Ray. You're not very good at lying, especially when it comes to me. You might as well tell me the truth because I will find out sooner rather than later."*

*"I met him at the pool hall through a friend. Later he said he needed a driver. That's what I do. End of story."*

*Deon had skimped out on a few crucial details. Yet, she knew that a tiny grain of truth lay in there somewhere. For now, she would take what she could get. At least now, he did not have to dodge her anymore. The truth had to come out, no matter how pretty or ugly it would later become. In whatever form it came in, she just had to accept it.*

## Chapter 7

Jacquelyn kept her promise to discuss her new opportunity over lunch with Will. She humored him by actually showing up to the office that Monday morning for a grand tour. "Okay, this is the main lobby. Here is the boardroom." Jacquelyn watched and listened as Will gave her a tour of just about every square foot of the building. Out of the many years they had known each other it was hard to believe that the first time she stepped into his family's pride and joy. After much deliberation, Jacquelyn decided to take Will's offer to be the company's newest editor. Even after accepting the position she still questioned if she had made the best decision after hearing what some of her new co-workers thought. Will proudly showed her off to the secretaries in the front office. "These lovely ladies help us keep Jacobs Publishing running. Don't know what we'd do without them." Jacquelyn introduced herself to Iris, Joyce, and Claire.

"Hi Jacquelyn," they said sweetly like a small choir. As soon as she and Will were out of hearing range, they began chatting. "Since when do new employees get a personal tour of the entire building by Mr. Jacobs?

"I know I didn't. Honey, I got lost on my first day, and no one held my hand."

"I guess we know what it takes to get the grand tour." They continued as Will and Jacquelyn moved further away from what he referred to as "The Hen House". The name was a perfect title because they did sound like a bunch of hens clucking away.

Maybe they said it on purpose so they could shake me, she thought. Jacquelyn had dealt with loud mouths clucking before, and these three would not be any different.

"And this is the most important office of them all."

Jacquelyn stood before a solid oak door with a gold nameplate reading: William A. Jacobs. The office was furnished with a solid mahogany desk and beautiful cream drapery. A gorgeous rug embellished the white marble floor. The room was huge, but it had a cozy feel to it. The surface of his desk was simply decorated with a tri-fold picture frame. He went around the desk to show her what each frame held. One had an early photo of his parents in front of a small brick building. He explained, "Those are my parents at the building that gave birth to Jacobs Publishing. My mom was his secretary, editor, photographer, and who knows what else." The other was a photo of him and Jacquelyn.

"Oh my God, you still have this picture. That was the day after I had my braces taken off," she said, barely containing her embarrassment, which showed through her blushing cheeks. "Why doesn't the last one have anything in it?" she questioned.

"For future plans," he said. "This used to be my father's office, but he handed it over to me when he named me the editor."

"Where is his new office?"

"His new office is at home. It's supposed to be less stress there. I know my parents. If I'm right, my mom is driving him *crazy, and he's returning the favor. The office next door was mine, but now it will be occupied by someone better suited, Ms. Hart. I'll miss it. I'll settle for this space, though," he said sarcastically. "Until you get comfortable with your surroundings, you'll learn the ropes here. I'll introduce you to our photographers this afternoon."*

*"Ha! That should keep the ladies downstairs chirping for a while."*

*"Don't pay them any mind. They talk about everyone, even me. Believe me, they quit chirping as soon as payday comes because I'm the one who signs the checks," he said.*

*"Do you train every new employee one on one?"*

*"Not really, but I am allowed to make some exceptions."*

*"How many exceptions have you made recently?" she asked. He paused, and she continued, "That many? And here I am thinking I'm special."*

*"So far, just one stubborn lady. I love her, though. She puts up with me."*

*"She loves you too, boss."*

*"I think Mr. Jacobs will be fine."*

*"Whatever, Anthony, yeah, I know what the A on your nameplate stands for."*

*An older woman opened the door and interrupted their moment.*

*"Excuse me, Mr. Jacobs. The printer is on the line for you."*

*"Thank you, Mrs. Johnson. Oh, I didn't get a chance to introduce the two of you. Hang on, let me take this call." Mrs.*

*Johnson did not waste any time getting acquainted with Jacquelyn.*

*"Hi sweetie, I'm Jane Johnson. You can call me Janie. You're a pretty little girl. I bet you'll keep the hen house on their toes."*

*"That part of the office is really known as the hen house?" Jacquelyn asked, fully amused.*

*"Oh yes, baby, be grateful you don't have to bother with them. As long as I've been here, we've called it that, and we call it that for a reason."*

*Janie must have been there since the day Jacobs Publishing opened. She was an older woman in her sixties, heavyset with a kind yet bold enough voice to match her ample frame.*

*"I'm happy I'll be in such great company," said Jacquelyn.*

*"If you need anything, ask Janie. I'm right out front," she said, smiling and closing the door. Will's phone call ended, and he proceeded with his deferred conversation.*

*"Okay, back to my tour. I'm glad you got a chance to meet Janie. She's like our mother around here. She always looks out for me."*

*"She's nice. I like her."*

*"Yeah, I can tell she likes you too. Trust me, if she didn't, you'd know already. Unlike too many people here, she*

*actually shows her true colors. Others come and go, but not Mrs. Johnson. She stays...like someone else, I hope."*

*"We'll see," she said.*

*"I was talking about Ms. Stevens down the hall," he said, teasing her.*

*"Maybe I should have Ms. Stevens come take my place," she said as if she were going to leave.*

*"No, no. Ms. Stevens looks more like Mr. Stevens. Your job is safe, especially from her," he laughed. Will briefed her on her role, and things went smoothly, that is, until Jacquelyn arrived home.*

*She came home to find a weepy Charlene sitting on the couch in the living room. Gwen was sitting next to her, trying to console her.*

*"What's going on?" asked Jacquelyn, sitting on Charlene's other side.*

*"My father locked me out of the house again. He found out I've been talking to my mama's sister. Thank God he doesn't know I've been looking for my mama. He acts like just because he hates her and her family that I have to feel the same. He told me that since I want to be around them so bad, I obviously don't need him anymore. Why do I have to be selfish in his eyes just because I want my family in my life too?" Gwen comforted her.*

*"It's okay, love. You'll be fine. We have our own drama to deal with before we go picking up stones to throw them your way. I'm surprised he can lift a finger to throw the first stone as much as he's messed up over the years." Jacquelyn noticed*

*Lena on the phone with her hands on her hips, waving her finger like a parent would do a disobedient child.*

*"Who is grandma talking to?"*

*"The stone thrower," answered Gwen. Lena's voice erupted,*

*"Don't worry, we'll take care of her ourselves God knows you won't!"*

*On that note, she slammed the phone down. She came to the living room where they were sitting. Her voice returned to its usual tone.*

*"No worries, sweetheart. You are welcome here."*

*"What does Deon have to say about the situation?" asked Jacquelyn.*

*"He left in a hurry right before I called her father. Queen, if you don't mind, I'd like to set Charlene up in your room. The back room is too cluttered to set her up in there tonight."*

*"I don't mind. It'll be like old times."*

*There was nothing new about Charlene having to visit their home because of her father's numerous outbursts. Over the years, the reasons behind is episodes may have changed, but the outcome was typically the same. Charlene's parents had terrible arguments when she was a child, and Jacquelyn's family always ushered her into their home. After Charlene's mother was gone, his aggressions transferred to disputes with his daughter. Lena always kept a watchful eye on their home, weary that one day their home might one day turn into a crime scene. Over the years there had been anonymous calls made to the authorities with concerns for Charlene, but* aside from a few visits nothing ever came of it. Her father knew how to make things appear as they should.

A fatigued Charlene decided to take a nap. The afternoon uproar had obviously drained her. Jacquelyn closed the bedroom door behind her carefully to avoid disturbing her. Jacquelyn entered the kitchen to hear the tail end of Gwen and Lena's conversation.

"I can't believe her father could be so heartless with her. We can clean out the back room tomorrow. She will be fine in there." Ray came into the door, looking puzzled.

"What's Deon doing at Charlene's house?" Ray had gone to the store before Jacquelyn returned home. He now came into a more peaceful atmosphere carrying two armfuls of groceries. "I saw Deon on her front porch talking to her father. Last thing I knew he was banned from over there."

"Lord, that boy is either crazy for stepping a foot over there being his prime target. Or maybe he's smarter than all of us if he can get through to that man. I don't want him snapping at my baby. I'm going over there," said Lena headed to the door.

"No. Wait, mama. Now think about what Deon says every day. I'm a man. I'm a man," said Gwen doing a poor impersonation of her nephew. She continued, "Now is the perfect time to prove it."

"If he's gone too long, we're going over there," said Lena.

"We'll see what the man comes up with," said Jacquelyn with the least bit of confidence in her brother. Like her grandmother, she too wanted to swoop down and protect Deon, but she knew Gwen was correct this time.

"He will be fine," added Ray reassuringly.

They trusted Ray's judgment. He was like a second father to Deon and Jacquelyn. If he thought Deon was in danger, he would have been the first person there. Ray may have been reserved, but there is nothing like a man when he feels like his family is being threatened. So, when Ray said that Deon would be fine, they assumed his attitude and knew everything would be as he stated.

About an hour later, Deon came through the door. His forehead glistened in the soft fluorescent light from perspiration. The only ones left waiting up for him were Jacquelyn and Lena. Gwen was getting Chris into bed, and Ray had already put himself to bed.

"Hey baby, are you okay?" asked Lena.

"I'm cool," said Deon. "Charlene isn't sleeping, is she?"

"She may be. It's been a long day."

He walked towards Jacquelyn's room,

"Well, she'll just have to wake up then."

Jacquelyn noticed his left fist was clenched tightly. "Chile it's been a long day. He should let her rest. I wonder what he's up to?" pondered Lena. "I don't know. I just hope it doesn't take long. I have to be at work early to start a new project. I should be in bed now, but let's state the obvious. We both wonder how that conversation with Charlene's father went." Jacquelyn tried to brush off the gut feeling that all was not well, but the only way she could was by getting to the truth.

*She thought about her brother's plans for California. She prayed that she would find that Deon and Charlene were still there in the morning. He came home with no clues to what had been discussed with Mr. Brown and no visible signs of him losing his composure on him. Jacquelyn understood that questioning her brother tonight would be futile. When she saw him exiting her room she decided not to waste her breath on trying to counsel or interrogate him. She just hugged him and for the first time in a while he let her. Before they parted ways she whispered, "If the weight of the world becomes too heavy for those shoulders of yours, I've got plenty room on mine to share your troubles." He nodded giving a slight smile.*

*Chapter 8*

*October 20, 1978 How did they grow up so fast? One day Deon's running in and out of the house, driving the family crazy worrying about him the next he's becoming a young man I can say I'm absolutely proud of. As mama would say, when your children are young they stay on your heels and when they're older they stay on your heart. I used to say Deon didn't have the sense God gave him. Turns out he had it the whole time and finally decided to use it. Whatever he'd said to Mr. Brown must have worked because he hadn't made any crazy visits here. He even waves to me every now and then. Only time will tell if this behavior will stick. Mr. Brown has yet to make amends with his own daughter. That's one stubborn man, and it's a shame too because his daughter is the only good thing he has done right. God has had his hands fixed on that child.*

*Deon had gone to Mr. Brown to ease Charlene's mind. Deon may not have had much respect left for her father, but he knew that making peace with him would make Charlene happy. He would say, "I'm in this for her, not anyone else."*

*When the family asked him about his conversation with Mr. Brown he gave no details, just a simple yet boastful, "I have a way with words."*

*"If that's how it is, then I need to take notes from you. Maybe I can keep your aunt quiet then," added Ray.*

*"I doubt it," said Deon.*

*Instead of going with her initial feelings, Jacquelyn went with the flow and allowed herself to be swept away along with everyone else. Life for Jacquelyn began to pick up at a steady pace as well. As she and Will worked together, she saw the businessman and the charming young man she had known for years function as one. Jacquelyn felt herself falling for him all over again. It was not like her to let things go or drop into order without having control. She liked this new feeling. She allowed herself to overlook the havoc that would soon take place at home. With her new found peace she tried to ignore the feeling in the pit of her stomach telling her to beware. Throughout most of her life anytime she hit a streak of happiness there was a hovering feeling of fear waiting for that happiness to come crashing down. Jacquelyn would take the joy that life handed her, but always with caution. It felt like her moment of happiness always seemed to come with a quick descend back to a reality where struggle seemed more normal than peace. However, this time she chose not to even acknowledge this feeling that had become way too familiar.*

*There was an abundance of scary thoughts of what if's Jacquelyn could entertain, but if Jacquelyn dwelt on those less inspiring things in her life, she would have never gotten a chance to grow. It was a decision that had its plus and minuses. It would later be up to her to see that the good was worth the bad. She learned from Lena that growth is not always pleasant, but it's always necessary in life.*

*Queen began to accept and to appreciate the transitions that came with this new chapter and whatever it brought along with it. Her new role at Jacobs Publishing brought its expected challenges. She literally walked through the door and had her position handed to her. With this show of favoritism came the routine catty remarks from a few female coworkers. From Jacquelyn's point of view the feelings of envy aimed towards her were fair, but she promised herself not to fall prey. The petty gossip would persist no matter her efforts of playing nice with the "Hen House." The discourse simply came with being the girlfriend of the boss. Despite her cold reception, minus Mrs. Johnson, she demanded that Will treat her like everyone else even with her unfair advantage. She reminded herself of this when he returned her articles filled with his extra critical critiques. And she finally allowed herself to settle into her office. One morning, Will entered her door, placing an old black and white photo of a couple on her desk. It looked like it had been taken in the nineteen-thirties, reminiscent of the young photographs of her grandparents.*

*"What a beautiful couple. Who are they?" asked Jacquelyn puzzled.*

*"They are our next cover story, Mr. and Mrs. Cullen. They have taken in foster children, even adopting two, for a span of over three decades. When we have the annual gala for*

*Jacobs Publishing, I thought that we should honor someone worthy of the praise."*

*The gala would celebrate the Jacobs' anniversary and officially introduce Will as the new executive editor. Jacquelyn was not surprised by this move of his. Will was never one for the limelight, and steering the attention elsewhere was very much like him.*

*"They're still around?" she asked, inspecting the picture of the handsome pair.*

*"They're not ancient baby, and yes they're still around. Their oldest daughter patched their story through to me, and I've heard their names through various associates. I thought that we could visit them and speak with them personally. They're still very active in the community."*

*"Alright, when do we meet them?"*

*"Now," he said, jingling his keys.*

*Even though Will was officially the boss, he liked to handle business with a hands-on approach. His father's intentions from day one were for Will to take command over his family's business. Regardless of his intentions he didn't allow his son to take any shortcuts starting him out in the mail room and allowing him to work his way up becoming an apprentice. Placing his legacy in Will's care gave him that much-needed peace of mind he needed in order to hand over the reins. Will was now training Jacquelyn to be his right hand, which didn't please his more tenured writers. Jacquelyn's presence and the resistance that it ushered in caused him to develop a balance. He was driven by his desire to avoid unraveling what his father had carefully built. He kept Jacquelyn by his side and an ear to ground to stay grounded.*

*They arrived at a quaint brick home with welcoming front porch. It was well kept without a leaf on the beautiful lawn. A teenage boy with a rake in one hand greeted them with the other.*

*Jacquelyn spoke, "Hi, we're here to speak with Mr. and Mrs. Cullen." He returned Jacquelyn's friendly smile before running off to get them.*

*"I see you have a fan," said Will.*

*"One of many," said Jacquelyn teasing.*

*"Keep in mind I'm the most important one."*

*"I'll try," she responded.*

*Mr. and Mrs. Cullen came from the front entrance of the house. They looked vital--the complete opposite of what Jacquelyn had expected. Mrs. Cullen was obviously baking because she had an apron covered with flour. Unfortunately, whatever she was baking was overpowered by the scent of Old Spice and aftershave worn by her husband. The smell did not bother Jacquelyn because it reminded her of her grandfather. Both couples introduced themselves and settled into a warm conversation. They spoke and enjoyed homemade cookies and cocoa in the living room. They reminisced on their experience as foster parents, highlighting the good and bad. Mr. Cullen had a distinct deep tone that held ones attention the moment he spoke. He was an excellent story teller, captivating every ear in the room. When he spoke, his baritone voice carried. He lowered it a* bit, apparently, so it would not reach the ears of their foster son who had greeted them.

"Lately, it's been hell trying to keep our youngest boys in line. We have Robert, twelve, and Tim whose, fourteen. You met Tim when you came earlier. They're both good boys. But Tim was having some problems in school before he came here about two years ago. After a while with us, he's been doing much better. Some of our former foster kids who are grown now stop in. From time to time, they mentor the kids. Then Tim started getting into fights again, saying he wanted to drop out of school. We know where it's coming from. One of our first foster kids came to visit too. He brings gifts and money to us. We don't take it, though," said Mr. Cullen. "He wants to play with dirty hands, then come here and think we don't see the messy trail behind him. He won't leave his dirty trail in this house. He's mad a name for himself in the streets and we want no parts of it."

"Even if it would help out around here," said his wife.

"It's one of those things we don't agree on," said Mr. Cullen, patting her hand.

"If you don't mind me asking, why won't you take the money?" asked Will.

"Fred isn't the nine to five job holding man. He lives off of easy money. But, if you ask me, there's nothing easy about sleeping with one eye open, constantly watching your back.

We don't accept dirty money in this house," he said with a sharp look towards his wife.

The name rang in Jacquelyn's ears. She repeated the name in her head, trying to jog her memory.

They ended their interview on a high note.

"Could I have you two pose right here by the fireplace?" Jacquelyn chose that spot because they had dozens of pictures of their foster children on their fireplace mantel. Trying to center them in the camera shot, she noticed one particular face.

"Let me guess this is Fred," she said, glancing at the younger version of a stranger who was becoming more uncomfortably familiar to her.

"Yes. How'd you know?"

"We've seen him around," she replied. Then, she went on with her work.

"Okay, right here. That's perfect." She took a few more shots before posing for some herself.

"A couple as cute as the two of you should be photographed," said Mrs. Cullen. Will held on to Jacquelyn's waist as Mrs. Cullen said, "Cheese."

Mr. Cullen only scratched the surface of Fred's history. They seemed old-fashioned, which meant that "easy money" or a dirty lifestyle could be from gambling to them. However, to Jacquelyn, there was much more to Fred than a gambler's hand. Jacquelyn shared with Will what she thought, and he gave her his take on it.

"I'd like to give Deon the benefit of the doubt, but you know him best. If he is involved in anything crazy, I don't want you to get caught up in it. If he says he can handle it, let him. He'll learn one way or another. If you keep interfering, he won't. Then he'll just resent what you're trying to do."

"Sounds like you had to learn that yourself."

"Except I was on the other side. My dad wanted to guide me in the company. I was hardheaded, though. Thought I knew it all, but after hitting my head a few times I learned after a while. I guess stubbornness runs in your family," he said, glancing at her.

"My family?" she scoffed.

"You're too stuck on mothering him."

"Fine, I'll cut the cord. He's on his own," she said with a cutting motion.

"Liar."

"At least you know me," she said.

They came off the elevator to find that their floor carried a heavy scent of lilacs. This scent was synonymous with Mrs. Jacobs. "

Well, I see my mother decided to pay us a visit."

"I'm not the only one who can't cut the cord." As she finished her statement, Mrs. Jacobs came from around the corner.

"Sweetheart, I was just looking for you and Jacquelyn," she said while hugging them.

"I wanted to personally invite you both to dinner next Saturday night, no excuses. Janie informed me of how hard the two of you have been working. Plus, it will allow us to catch up," she said, smiling.

Jacquelyn couldn't dodge her directly without trying to come up with a long, fabricated story. She hesitantly accepted the invitation while cringing at the thought of another snooty evening. The things I'll do for love, she thought.

Chapter 9

*The need to keep their families connected was one thing that Mrs. Jacobs and Lena had in common. Jacquelyn marked the date for the Jacobs' dinner, and before the ink dried on her calendar, Lena was organizing one of her own. Lena almost bought out the store trying to get the ingredients for everyone's favorite food.*

*"With everything that's been going on, a nice family dinner would be nice. I can't remember the last time we all sat down together," she said to Jacquelyn the night before her announcement for dinner. They all settled at the table, including Will, who she called and invited personally. A glance around the table, and people would think we were normal, thought Jacquelyn. Normal was so far from her family's description, especially recently. After everyone had been seated, Lena instructed Chris to turn off the television before they began.*

*"Baby, turn that thing off. We don't need to compete with that box for one another's attention." His finger barely touched the knob when Ray demanded that he stop.*

*"Wait, wait. I know that man." The man he was referring to was someone almost everyone at the table recognized. They all viewed the mug shot that was splashed across the screen. "Turn it up."*

*The reporter had everyone's attention.*

*"Thank you, John. We are live here at the scene where authorities have apprehended a man believed to be*

responsible for several swindling thousands of dollars from local business owners. He may also be connected to the multiple arsons in the area. The suspect, Fred Thomas, is believed to be not working alone. Those who know of any others connected with the suspect are asked to contact the police at this time."

The reporter went on with her story while Ray spoke over the TV.

"I would have never known Mr. Thomas was involved in something that deep. Man, this world is a trip. I'm glad I never put my money into any of those big investments Fred was always bragging about."

"Yes, Lord, you never know. Turn that TV off now, baby, and come to the table," said Lena.

Ray began the prayer. He asked that all eyes be closed, and heads bow. All heads may have been bowed, but every eye did not close. Jacquelyn's eyes met with her brother's. Will noticed and then slightly squeezed her hand so she wouldn't look obvious. Jacquelyn knew that her brother kept more than a minor detail or two to himself. She could no longer accept another evasive answer. Dinner could not end soon enough. Jacquelyn stuffed food into her mouth instead of savoring it.

"Queen slow down. You'll get indigestion, not to mention you're looking like a little piglet in front of Will. I hope

Queen's eating habits aren't disturbing you are they, honey?" asked Lena after looking at her granddaughter.

"Oh no, ma'am, it's fine. I've learned to appreciate her healthy appetite," he said while rubbing her back.

After dinner, Jacquelyn walked Will out to the front porch. The crisp October wind swept over the two huddled together on the steps. Outside of her grandmother Will was the first person she could reveal herself to without feeling vulnerable. She never felt guilty for overexposing herself or wished that she had held back. Jacquelyn exhaled slowly and watched as the cold air mimicked puffs of smoke. They stood silently for a moment then Jacquelyn verbalized the jumble in her head, hoping that Will could make better sense of it.

"I don't know how to talk to him anymore. I know we've both grown, but it's more than that. When I look at him, a bunch *of question marks appear. He'll shut down on me if I say anything with the smallest hint of negativity."*

*"It's understandable. You're used to him just being your baby brother. Now he's going to be someone's..."*

*"Accomplice. Someone's accomplice," she said, interrupting him.*

*"Sweetheart, you don't know anything for certain. Give the man a break."*

*"But I do know my brother for certain. Maybe the problem is I've been giving him too many breaks. You saw him at the table. You saw guilt written all over that boy's face."*

*"Maybe it wasn't guilt," said Will.*

*"What then if it's not guilt?" she asked.*

*"Fear. He could have heard something he wasn't supposed to hear while he was driving Fred around."*

*"It's possible, but that doesn't answer everything."*

*They paused, hearing footsteps come to the door. Deon walked through the door.*

*"Hey, I gotta make a run. Charlene's getting a cold, and we're out of medicine."*

*Will made small talk while Jacquelyn looked Deon up and down. X-ray and mind reading could have come in handy, but she worked with some scouring expressions she learned from* watching Gwen. Finally, Deon departed, leaving behind a distraught Jacquelyn.

"Later," said Will slapping his hand in return. Then, when Deon had driven away, Will said to her, "I hope you never look at me like that."

"Oh, you noticed," said Jacquelyn.

"I was trying to ignore it," he said.

"Good, that means my brother noticed too."

"You can't scare him into talking to you. You're not kids anymore. But if he's dealing with a person like Fred, I'm sure your scare tactics need to catch up. No more avoiding it. Just have a real conversation with him."

"That's the best advice you've given me."

"You tend to be a little hardheaded, so my advice is limited. It's always here, though," he said after kissing her good night. "See you Saturday for dinner?"

"Ugh. I don't know if I can make it through another family dinner without wanting to reach across the table and hurt the person sitting in front of me. One of those stuck-up dinner guests may push me to that point," said Jacquelyn.

"You'll make it," he said, laughing. He didn't know she was serious despite the smile on her face. They said their goodbyes. Jacquelyn closed the door behind her shaking the cold off of her body. She walked past the back room to see if Charlene was awake, and fortunately she was.

"Hey do you mind if we talk?"

"Of course not. What's wrong?" said Charlene seeing the concern through the lines on her friend's forehead.

"Well, I don't know yet. Did Deon tell you where he was going?"

"Oh, umm. Yeah, he...I need something for my sore throat, and he ran out for me."

"Hmm. That's interesting that he couldn't find anything from that mini drugstore in Grandma's pantry," said Jacquelyn.

Charlene looked dumbfounded and then tried to recover her story. "You know he probably forgot to check."

Jacquelyn rolled her eyes.

"You two are the worst liars ever! Look, you and Deon both know more than you're telling me...So spill it."

Charlene looked around as if the walls had ears or eyes and reached behind Jacquelyn to close the door. "Deon knows the man we saw on the news," said Charlene.

"That part I knew already. I coincidentally met his foster parents because we're doing a cover story for the magazine. Deon is his driver when he comes to Uncle Ray's," said Jacquelyn trying to speed up the process. "He's not just

*Fred's driver on the clock." Jacquelyn looked at her and frowned.*

*"So, are you saying that Deon was a driver for some of those scams?"*

*"Possibly," answered Charlene hesitantly.*

*Then, almost afraid to learn the answer, she asked, "Charlene, please be honest with me. Did he have anything to do with the arsons?"*

*Neither of them wanted to equate Deon with the terrible things Fred had done, but they knew everyone would assume that he was guilty by association.*

*"He only drove Fred a few times, and no one got hurt. I don't know every single detail, but I know your brother. He got out of it because he didn't want to get caught up in that drama."*

*"He could be caught up in a lot more than drama. Fred is in serious trouble. Where did my brother really go tonight?"*

*"He got a call from one of Fred's friends," said Charlene.*

*"And he actually went?"*

*"What was he supposed to do? If he didn't go to them, they would come to him. They know where we live and where he works,"*

*"How could he be this careless?"*

*"At times he was like an open book, and other times, he could be like a locked and buried chest. He didn't mean to be*

careless. He just, I don't know," even Charlene, Deon's biggest fan, could not come up with one valid answer.

Jacquelyn picked up where she left off. "He never means to. I can't get him out of this." She paused, "That explains how he knew I was related to Uncle Ray."

"You met him?"

"Will and I took Chris to the park. He wandered off, and Fred found him. He knew I was Uncle Ray's niece before I said a word. He said he recognized Chris from the office when Aunt Gwen brought him," said Jacquelyn.

"Wait. As far as I know, Chris has only been to Ray's office once when it opened. I watch him when he comes home."

"Well, like you said, he knows where he lives."

"I know it looks bad, but..."

"Charlene, there is no but. He knows better than this. If my Grandma finds out, it'll break her heart. And really, what was he thinking?"

"Your brother can tell you better than I can. He started before Ray gave him a job. He'd just found out about California, and Fred offered him money here and there for favors. If he said that he didn't harm anybody, I believe him. He got himself into this mess and is smart enough to get out of it." Jacquelyn shook her head in disbelief at how naïve she could be. Charlene would still believe him even if she caught him in the act. Charlene went on to explain the situation to her friend.

"Fred is more than some random guy to me. He's played a bigger part in my life more than you know. He's the man that *caused my family to crumble. Fred is the man that my mother had an affair with." Stunned, Jacquelyn's face asked the question that her lips would not allow her to. Why would Charlene want anything to do with the reason behind her family's demise? "Queen, you may think I'm crazy for dealing with him, but I was desperate. He's been able to help me put the pieces of what really happened back then together. And because of him, I've been able to reconnect with my mother. He told me where my mother went after my daddy made her leave."*

*"So, what does Fred get out of this? He doesn't come off as the giving and no strings attached kind of person."*

*"In some way, I guess he has a conscience. He says he always felt bad for what happened to my mom. They ended things but managed to remain close over the years. He knew we'd need the funds to make it to California, so he offered Deon a job before Ray. He would point out the weak links, the people who easily fall for Fred's scheme. Fred would do the rest, though. Deon never directly hurt anyone."*

*Jacquelyn sighed, "Directly is the key. He still played a role. I doubt Fred's conscience motivated him to offer a helping hand."*

*"I'm sure you want to help, but if you step in, you could be doing more harm than good. This is my chance to finally find my mom and get back a small piece of what was taken from*

me. Even if it means getting assistance from someone as rotten as Fred, so be it."

"Okay. Thanks for being so open with me. I'll talk to him later," was all Jacquelyn could add.

"Oh, please don't tell Deon that I told you anything. Then he won't tell me anything else."

"I won't," promised Jacquelyn.

She went to her room and was bombarded with her thoughts and worries. Since her grandmother was asleep, she called the next person on her list. She listened as the phone rang, wondering if she should hang up each time a ring went unanswered. He's probably asleep by this time. He's the bedtime of a grandpa. I'm gonna hang up, thought Jacquelyn. When she was about to take the phone receiver away from her ear, she heard a sluggish "Hello." Realizing it was Jacquelyn, Will cleared most of the sleep out of his voice.

"Hey baby, everything okay?" She filled him in on the latest news. He then gave her a few comforting words. "If it makes you feel any better, I'll keep my lawyer on hand for Deon."

"Lawyer, do you think it'll go that far?"

"If your brother has anything to do with this or knows anything surrounding it, trouble won't be far behind. He'll need someone to speak for him besides his big sister."

"Well, that does make me feel better."

"You get some rest," said Will.

Jacquelyn wished that her mind could've gone along with her body and listened to him. While her body slipped into slumber, her mind rebelled. She dreamt that she was a little girl playing with Deon. They were there at their grandmother's home alone. She spotted her brother running to the backroom. She ran behind him, but he wasn't there when she entered the room. A little girl came out and screamed, "You found me!" barely containing her giggles. She reminded Jacquelyn of her mother with a huge smile and familiar eyes. Jacquelyn tried to question the girl, but her attempts were futile. The girl only ran away as Jacquelyn tripped and fell into the darkness. The morning brought headlines and new games of hide-n-seek. Finally, Ray came to the kitchen table with the newspaper. Fred's arrest and mug shot was front-page news. "Baby no garbage before breakfast. You know, that's a bunch of hype. The papers know about as much as we do...which is nothing. Do something more constructive with that paper," said Gwen.

"Like what?"

"We could use fire. Light a flame. After all, isn't he known for setting fires too?"

Good, the less they know, the better, thought Jacquelyn.

"It is chilly in here," he said, rubbing his hands together. He started a fire in fireplace, and Jacquelyn watched as the article crumbled from the flames. God please don't let this be a sign of Deon's life going up in smoke.

"Queen come help Charlene set the table," instructed Gwen.

"You know Deon was his driver. Fred always requested him. Where is that boy anyway? He's usually the first one at the table," said Ray.

"I walked by his room a minute ago. He's sleeping in late. A long night I guess. Too long if you ask me," said Gwen looking over at Charlene. She continued, "Honey if I were you, I'd have plenty of questions, and if he knew what was good for him, he'd have some answers!"

Ray spoke, "Well, you aren't her. Thankfully, there's only one of you."

"Amen," chimed in Lena. Charlene and Jacquelyn knew partially knew the answer to about last night, but they still had many more questions about his other nights. "And let me add a Hallelujah to that," said Deon carrying Chris on his shoulders. "We thought you were gonna sleep the whole day away," said Lena.

"I woke him up!" said Chris proudly.

Breakfast went well for the most part. The clanking of forks onto plates made up for the absence of words. Jacquelyn held her tongue and thought of a way to confront Deon without causing an uproar in the family. Things had been so peaceful lately. Gwen and Ray were for actually happy for the first time in years, work was going better than Jacquelyn could imagine, and Lena was in pure bliss as any Matriarch could be her family's lack of discord.

"We'll leave the clean-up for the gentlemen. We've got to find the perfect dress for Queen," said Lena.

A perfect little black dress, you can't go wrong. Jacquelyn lived by this rule, or instead, had taken the idea and ran with it. Elle's Boutique had a vast collection of black dresses, and Jacquelyn had selected all of them. Gwen made it her mission to clear her niece of this unofficial rule.

"Queen, are you going to a celebration or a funeral? Black dresses are fine for other occasions, but you want more. Add *some color to your life girl. Let me see that," Gwen said, grabbing an armful of "drab" dresses as she put it. "That one isn't too bad," she said, returning one of the dresses to her niece.*

*"What about that one? It's cute," said Jacquelyn, pointing to another dress now in her Aunt's arms. "It's cute, but you want a gown that'll stun them. You want to keep your man's eyes on you all night." Lena and Charlene watched as Gwen took over.*

*Lena whispered to her, "This ought to be good. The two of them agree on something. Pigs must be flying!" Gwen went from each aisle, shuffling and pulling at a few outfits here and there.*

*"Okay, try these on," she said, handing the gowns to Jacquelyn. She thought about searching for more but remained confident in her selection. Then her eyes were caught by a striking dress in the window. A flowing ruby gown was displayed on a mannequin that could not showcase it as Jacquelyn could.*

*"That's the one. Excuse me, miss. Could I please see that dress over there?" she asked the salesgirl.*

*"We usually don't sale those gowns that are on display," answered the girl whose name tag read Pam.*

*"What's the point of putting it up for display if you can't buy it?" asked Gwen with an attitude.*

*"All of our dresses are one of a kind meaning only one of them. We have to put something on our mannequins to draw*

our customers in," Pam said, returning the same attitude Gwen had given her.

"Well, Pam, that one has done its job. I'm a customer and I was drawn in." They bickered back and forth.

Finally, Jacquelyn stepped out of the dressing room. "What's going on?" Her Aunt paused from her dispute to see her.

With her hands on her hips, Gwen said, "I stand corrected. That's the one."

Jacquelyn adorned a cream and golden gown that flowed yet hugged her body beautifully. "You can keep that one," said Gwen walking away from Pam. She glared at Gwen, and then gave a sweet smile to the rest of them as she rang up the gown. Gwen gave herself more credit than she deserved on the way home.

"See, Queen, I knew I'd find you the perfect gown. It's much better than one of those dull dresses you were about to get. That one brings you to life!"

"Maybe I would've gotten it cheaper because of this tear at the bottom if you didn't have to argue with the sales girl."

"What rip? You should have spoken up. Maybe you could've gotten a discount. You need to start speaking up like me," said Gwen.

"Before you two start going back and forth, I'll end it. I can fix the rip," said Lena.

They pulled closer to the house and saw a police car leaving the driveway. Jacquelyn's stomach started to sink at the *thought of her brother sitting in the back of the cop car being driven away.*

*"Lord Jesus, let me see what's happening. Gwen, help Charlene get the bags out of the car."*

*They followed Lena into the house. Ray was at the kitchen table when she approached him. "Ray, why were the police here?" asked Lena. "*

*They said that they had to ask me a few questions about Fred Thomas since he was a former client of mine. They asked me about my history with him. It was nothing. Everyone relax now. Come on and sit down. I just made a fire," he said, welcoming them in. He calmed their nerves, knowing that there was more behind the cop's visit than he made it seem. Jacquelyn sat near her grandmother, contemplating what would happen in her family's life. None of what she could come up with came close to what awaited them.*

*Chapter 10*

*Jacquelyn read the next diary entry. Unlike the others, it had no date, and it was shorter than all of the others. However, it was a Bible verse that related to the days ahead for the Harts.*

*"For there is nothing covered, that shall not be revealed; neither hid, that shall not be known." Luke 12:2*

*"Okay, almost there. Aah, I got it," said Charlene. She zipped Jacquelyn into her dress. "Make sure you don't eat too much. You don't want to pop out of your dress before the second course."*

*"Wouldn't that be a site? That would fuel the conversations of those "sophisticated ladies" for weeks. They'd probably be saying I'm too poor to afford a good dress," said Jacquelyn.*

*"Don't worry, Queen, you'd look better than them even if you wore a garbage bag."*

*Charlene looked at the clock on the wall, sighing, and saying "Is that clock right?" Jacquelyn looked at it as well.*

*"Yes. At least, it was the last time I checked it. Got big plans tonight?"*

*"No, but Deon was supposed to be home by now," answered Charlene. Jacquelyn checked her wristwatch to make sure that she was correct to reassure her. Doing the math in her head, she calculated that Ray's office had closed two hours ago. The pool hall was closed due to renovations. Other than that, his whereabouts were a mystery to them. Deon's circle of friends these days seemed to be shadow lurkers. The kids*

that he had recently graduated with had gone in all directions with some going away to college, a few going to the military, and sadly a couple finding themselves behind bars after one too many bad decisions. Lena had set aside money for both he and Jacquelyn to go school. Deon opted to go trade school to become an electrician, but his role as apprentice ended abruptly after he decided he knew more than the instructor. Deon's greatest downfall was always himself. The argument between had been one for the books. Jacquelyn remembered Lena screaming at Deon, something she rarely did, as Gwen was known as the family's loud mouth. After the explosive argument Lena promised to allow Deon to become the man that he wanted to be without any interference. "My prayers are the only thing that I offer you. I hope that they cover you," she told him after their argument. As Lena relented Jacquelyn felt the need to double down on her commitment to watch out for her brother. Her relationship was the only buffer between Jacquelyn's brother and her need to monitor his daily life. "You seem worried," said Jacquelyn. The phone rang, disturbing them.

"It's probably that prank caller. They've been calling all day. We pick up, and then, after a few seconds, they hang up. It's driving us crazy!" said Charlene. "My guess is it's a bunch of kids behind it. Don't let them drive you up a wall. You've got more important things to think about." Jacquelyn knew Charlene wasn't naive enough to believe it was a random call. One moment he says that he doesn't know too much about that whole Fred Thomas case. The next minute he's all nervous about it. I don't even think he sleeps at night," said Charlene.

"If he doesn't know anything, what does he have to worry about?"

"I don't know much these days. My focus is California. We're so close. We've both been working really hard to save money for the move. I can't see him getting caught up so easily. I'm going to start school once we get settled. I found a local community college and Deon even said he would start too," Charlene beamed as she imagined her future.

"That sounds like a good plan," Jacquelyn smiled back at her friend. She wished that she could share in her optimism, but in her heart she felt like her dear friend's vision wouldn't come as easy as she hoped that it would. The doorbell rang. "That's Will. Okay, Grandma should be home from Mrs. Wilson's any minute, and it's across the street anyway. Aunt Gwen and Uncle Ray will be back from dinner soon too. I've already put Chris to bed. I wrote down Will's parent's number. And don't even stress over that knucklehead," she said, referring to her brother. "Oh yeah, Mrs. Wilson's number is in the address book if you need it."

"Jacquelyn, I'll be fine. I'm not some broken little bird. Don't worry," said Charlene.

"Sorry. It's a force of habit," said Jacquelyn.

"Go before Will leaves. Have fun."

"Thanks," said Jacquelyn scurrying to the door. She slowed down her pace, trying to glide with grace like Lena. She *opened the door letting in a rush of icy cold air from outside. The wind blew her hair out of place.*

*Will fixed it, "Are we ready now?"*

*"Yes, we are," she responded confidently. They settled into the car, and Jacquelyn caught her breath. Will looked over at her and spoke before she had a chance.*

*"Tonight, no problems or issues will be mentioned. I won't talk about work, and you won't talk about family."*

*"It's sad that those two topics bring so much grief," said Jacquelyn.*

*"That's my point. I left my worries at the office, and you'll leave yours at the doorstep. Deal?" asked Will.*

*"Deal," agreed Jacquelyn.*

*They pulled into the driveway as Jacquelyn took a deep breath saying to herself, "I'm the Queen, and they're just peasants." Her brother would say it to mock her when they were younger, but Jacquelyn would use it whenever she needed a boost of assurance. She later learned to use it to her advantage. Mrs. Jacobs answered the door.*

*"Hello, darlings," she said, hugging each of them. "Ooh, come in," she said as she caught a chill from the wind. Jacquelyn found no loud music, and surprisingly no entourage or partygoers were present. Jacquelyn exhaled with relief. They*

*followed Mrs. Jacobs into the dining room, which was arranged immaculately.*

*"Mrs. Jacobs, your dining room is gorgeous," said Jacquelyn gushing over its perfection.*

*"Thank you, sweetheart. I recently did a little remodeling since the last time you were here," she said, smiling.*

*Mr. Jacobs appeared, saying, "Yes, my wife has great taste, expensive, but great. She has even better taste in men. Well, besides herself, Will had to get his looks somewhere," he said with a chuckle. "You should see her side of the family," he said, playfully teasing.*

*"Careful dear, there's a reason why you don't see any of your family member's pictures framed," said his wife jokingly. Their lighthearted banter was nothing compared to the venomous quarrels Jacquelyn witnessed growing up between Gwen and Frank. They all laughed as they were seated at the massive dining room table. Will and Mr. Jacobs chatted about the subject that they connected on best, work, while Mrs. Jacobs scurried back to the kitchen to bock off more orders to cook. Jacquelyn gazed around the room imagining all of the exquisite meals and underwhelming conversations this table must have held. Moments later Mrs. Jacobs reentered the room followed by the maid bringing out dinner.*

*"I hear you kids are doing exceptionally well, in particular the magazine. More importantly, I see that the two of you are*

doing well together," said Mr. Jacobs referencing their bond. He pulled out a framed magazine cover.

"Our first cover together," said Will like an giddy little boy, meeting Jacquelyn's eyes. He grasped her hand with excitement.

"I'm proud of both of you. I know that my company is safe," said Mr. Jacobs raising his glass for a toast. The glasses gently clanked together as Jacquelyn sipped, taking the moment in. "Any idea of what your next cover story will be?"

Mrs. Jacobs stopped him, "Bruce, they did not come here for a business meeting. Let them enjoy their time off." He tried his best to stay away from the subject of work, but he couldn't. His company was like another child in the way that he loved it. While father and son spoke about the anniversary gala Jacquelyn and Mrs. Jacobs' conversation centered around the fashion possibilities and guests.

"I still have to find my jewelry to wear with my gown. As a matter of fact, I have some jewelry that would look lovely on you," said Mrs. Jacobs. Jacquelyn didn't have a chance to properly thank her before because she received an impromptu call.

The maid approached Jacquelyn saying, "Excuse me, Ms. Hart, you have a phone call. Her first thoughts of panic went to Deon. I knew I should have stayed home, thought Jacquelyn as she followed the maid to the kitchen. The once heavenly aroma wafting from the kitchen now made her *stomach queasy. She placed the phone against her ear. "Hello," said Jacquelyn softly.*

*Gwen's voice blared from the other end of the phone. "Queen, you need to get home if you can. Your brother has been arrested."*

*"I'm on my way," said Jacquelyn slamming the phone down. She came to the living room, where everyone was enjoying their meal. Remaining calm, she said, "Mr. and Mrs. Jacobs, I've had a wonderful time, but I have to excuse myself. I have a family emergency. I really do apologize."*

*"Sweetheart no problem. Please let us know if everything is okay," said a concerned Mrs. Jacobs. Will walked her to the car quickly. He looked over at Jacquelyn.*

*"It's your brother, isn't it?" he asked.*

*"Yeah, Gwen was the one who called. I knew before she said a word it was serious. He was arrested, and I'm pretty sure it wasn't for a traffic violation. It reeks of Fred." She shook her head in disgust. Her fear for her brother's safety had been replaced with anger for his naive nature. She replayed all of the instances when he turned her away, telling her he was fine. The compassion that she felt for Deon gradually flipped to resentment.*

*"I'll call my attorney's office as soon as I get home. Don't worry, baby," said Will.*

*"Right now, I'm less concerned with what the cops or what anyone else is going to do to him. They should be worried about what I'm about to do to him. This is the last thing our family needs right now," Jacquelyn rolled her eyes. Usually, when Jacquelyn was upset, Will would counter it by saying,*

"You're too pretty to be mad," but he knew that she would not take the comment well at the moment.

"We'll take care of this together," said Will holding her hand. When they reached the house, Ray was looking pitiful on the porch steps.

"Hey, Uncle Ray."

"Hey, Queen."

"What do we have to do from here? Deon was arrested?" she asked. Uncle Ray and Lena seemed like bottomless pits full of wisdom and advice. However, lately, they both came up short on those wise words that usually flowed so instinctively.

"As far as we know they took him in for questioning. I already went down to the police department. I guess your Aunt called you when I was there. She didn't have to interrupt your night because of your hard-headed brother. I'm not sure how long they're going to hold him for questioning. It'll be—interesting to see how we get him out of *this one. I thought giving him a job would help avoid a situation like this."*

*"Ray, I have a lawyer if this situation comes to that. I'll take care of the costs," said Will.*

*"Thanks, Will. I really appreciate your help. I'll pay you back as soon as possible," said Ray. He paused, then said, "No. Deon is going to repay you as well."*

*"Ray, it's fine. I'll..."*

*"No. I appreciate your gesture, but it's time that he really starts being held accountable," said Ray firmly.*

*"Uncle Ray how did they even think to look in Deon's direction?" asked Jacquelyn.*

*"They originally came here to ask him a few questions about Mr. Thomas because someone mentioned Deon's name, but you know Deon. Like his Aunt, he had to get smart and start running off at the mouth. They claim they know he's associated with Fred, and some witness recognized him from one of the scams Fred pulled. Your aunt and Charlene were a mess in there. I had to get some space to get things together." Ray stood up and shook Will's hand. "I think I have it together now," he said, walking inside. Will studied Jacquelyn's face as she stared into the sky, wondering what would come next.*

*"How about we take Monday off?" said Will.*

*"Okay," said Jacquelyn sighing heavily. Usually, Jacquelyn would have objected. She never liked her brother or anyone*

else' antics disrupt her, but she had to be there for her family.

"Do you want me to stay?" he asked.

"No, and yes, but I'll go with no because I think it would be better to handle this nut house solo. Thanks for tonight. It was nice to get away from the madness, even if it was for a couple of hours," said Jacquelyn.

"It was my pleasure. It's easier said than done, but get some sleep. I'm sure you'll need it."

"Oh, I plan on sleeping like a baby. I'm tired of allowing my brother's messes to become yet another sleepless night for me. This is the last straw." Although her lips meant everything she said, her heart protested against each word. Jacquelyn felt herself getting heated. Finally, she calmed down to say, "I love you. Good night."

Walking into the house, she felt comforted by Will's support and wished to give someone the same feeling of comfort. However, almost every door was closed except for one. The light that normally exuded from each room was shut off from the closed door. The darkness made the hallways extra dark and took away from the warmth that usually engulfed the Hart home. Jacquelyn remembered what Lena said about closed doors. She wondered what these doors would say about her family. She walked into her grandmother's room. Lena was awake reading her Bible. She had not dropped her routine because of the latest family drama. She heard the floors creak as her granddaughter moved closer.

"Hey, Queen," she said without looking up from her Bible.

"How'd you know it was me?" asked Jacquelyn.

"As much as you all come in and out of here, I've learned the difference. Come and sit with me," said Lena as she placed her Bible on her nightstand.

Jacquelyn hopped out of her coat and shoes leaving them on the floor. She jumped under the covers, pulling them up to her neck, and rested her head on her grandmother's arm. Lena looked down at Jacquelyn and then smiled.

"Underneath all that makeup, you're still my baby. When it comes to my other baby...." Lena shook her head. "What do we do about him?"

"I've been trying to figure that out since the day Momma and Daddy brought him home from the hospital. I still haven't figured it out yet," said Jacquelyn.

"Ever since you and your brother were kids, he has been determined to run at his own pace, and you have been trying to keep him in line."

"That's why I don't understand any of this. Lately, I haven't been able to control what he's been doing."

"That's the problem. Queen we can't control what goes on in our own lives, let alone anyone else's. It's up to Deon to decide what goes on in his life. As much as we'd like to protect the ones we love, some incidents are going to happen *as they may. He allowed certain errors to occur, so now he, and unfortunately, Charlene, have to live with it."*

*"How is Charlene?" asked Jacquelyn.*

*"It obviously hurt her, but she's strong. I think she knew it was leading up to this."*

*"You seem to be taking the whole situation a whole lot better than I expected," said Jacquelyn.*

*"Well, I handed it over to the Lord. Honey, if I worried about everything that goes on in this house, I'd have a head white as snow like my sisters. Worrying constantly won't change what it is."*

*"I think I'll be sleeping here tonight," said her granddaughter, snuggling up beside her. "Fine by me," said Lena smiling.*

*With Jacquelyn's mind centered on her brother Charlene's welfare had fallen short. Unfortunately, Charlene knew more than what she was saying. When Jacquelyn looked at the entire situation, she knew she could only hold Deon responsible for his role in this disaster.*

## Chapter 11

*The next day Will kept her company as they waited for Ray to return home with Deon. Lena cooked to keep herself occupied. She used food as a remedy for all things. If it was a headache, she suggested tea, stomach aches, her special stew, and broken hearts called for her blend of spices tied into her secret drink recipe. Every family member had their thirst quenched at least once through that drink.*

*"I love my brother, yet who's to say he won't do something stupid again. All of this stress will have been for nothing."*

*"I can't believe his main defendant is turning on him," said Will.*

*"I'm not turning on him I'm just being logical."*

*"Life doesn't always go off of logic. Who's to say he won't do better," said Will.*

*"We can't go off of false hope for him. Uncle Ray and the rest of us can't keep giving ourselves headaches all because we're trying to think of a way to help him out, knowing he'll turn around and do the same thing again."*

*"I'd like to be as optimistic as you. We'll have to watch this play out," said Will. They heard a car door slam. Chris stood on his toes to peer out of the window.*

*"Deon and Daddy are home," announced Chris. The two of them came through the door, neither wearing a smile. Ray had a serious look on his face. The vein in his forehead was*

*present. It only appeared after an argument or when he was really angry.*

*"Hey, welcome home. I cooked your favorite meal. Meatloaf, mashed potatoes, greens, and pound cake for dessert," said Lena.*

*"I'm not hungry. Maybe later," said Deon speaking sluggishly.*

*Gwen must have had a special antenna to sense when drama was around. She called her son over to her. "Chris, come help Mommy color in your room. Come on, baby," she said, walking with him to his room and closing the door behind them. Ray shook his head disapprovingly at Deon's nonchalant attitude.*

*"I've never seen somebody that ungrateful," Ray said, clenching his teeth.*

*"Look, I said thank you. I could've stayed in there if I wanted to be hassled," said Deon stubbornly. He turned his back against his uncle as he began to walk out of the room. Jacquelyn was taken aback by the behavior of her brother. No appreciation or remorse could be found in his tone. Instead, she and Will saw the rage built in Ray as it rained upon Deon. Ray grabbed him by the collar and slammed him against the wall. Then, still clutching his nephew's collar, Ray let his emotions out.*

*"Boy, after all that, this family has gone through for you, and you want to come in here with that garbage! You're lucky your grandmother hasn't kicked your behind out on the streets. That woman is your saving grace, or else I would do*

*it myself." Deon tried to loosen his grip, but Ray pushed him back to the wall. "You want to be a man so bad...."*

*Deon interrupted him, "I am. In case you haven't noticed, you're not the only one trying to provide for this family."*

*"I'm not throwing away my family in the process! If you're set on being a man and taking care of your family, stop running scared and acting like a little boy. Yeah, son, I know they're not prank callers calling this house 'round the clock. Calling to see if you snitched! What, you don't have anything to say now?" Ray released Deon, and he remained silent. Ray turned his back to the other side of the wall to cool down.*

*Finally, Deon spoke, "I don't need a father anymore."*

*"You don't know what you need. Whether you like it or not, I will always be here for you and your sister. I don't care if I have to be your father while you're kicking and screaming like a spoiled brat. If it's not for you, it'll be for your parents. That's a promise I will keep," he said, storming off. Deon stood in the spot that Ray left him, motionless and fists tightened. Glaring in the direction where his Uncle stood.*

*Lena decided to give her input. She pointed towards Will and Ray, saying, "Those are the men you need to be imitating instead of some thug you don't know from a blade of grass. These people don't give a damn about you." She walked away as her silk robe waved behind her. Jacquelyn and Will were left with nothing to say to Deon. He went to Charlene's room, perhaps to speak his peace to her without receiving another speech.*

*"Is that a big hint for me to leave?" asked Will.*

*"Not quite yet. I could use your company tonight. That wasn't the homecoming anyone expected. What my uncle said was the truth though."*

*The couple made use of the blazing fire and finished the meal that was meant to welcome Deon. After their conversations led to a hush the couple fell asleep on the couch. Silence muffled their minds from the noise of harsh words and hurt feelings. However, the security was broken with a rude awakening to all who slept. A large brick came through the dining room window. Jacquelyn and Will were immediately shaken from their slumber at the sound of breaking glass and the hard thud of the wood crashing to the floor. Screeching tires were heard as the assailants left the scene. Ray was the first person to arrive in the dining room with a shotgun in hand. Gwen followed sleepily-eyed, carrying Chris, who clutched her tightly. Everyone else came after. Deon knew he was the reason behind the shattered peace, but he couldn't cover it up with a clever twist of the truth. No embellishment would work with the scene that he was responsible for. Ray looked over at his nephew, waiting for him to speak from his guilty conscience.*

*"It's some of Fred's boys," said Deon.*

*"If they really wanted to do damage, it wouldn't have been just a brick flying through the window. They did it to scare*

*us. You all go back to bed. I'll take care of it," said Ray, regaining the house's attention.*

*Will helped Ray and Deon clean as Jacquelyn made the couch more comfortable for him in the living room. Lena wouldn't allow him to leave because of what had just happened. To give her peace of mind, Will complied.*

*The next morning evidence of the previous night was still present. Although, fragments of the broken glass had been swept away, Ray and the others boarded up the window until it could be repaired later. It would be nice if feelings could be as easily mended. Apologies were made. Kind words would be exchanged. Yet, accepting and dismissing words spoken with passion and anger took time. Forgiveness and maturity, along with time, had to be applied to the wounds to ensure proper healing.*

*Jacquelyn opted to go to work instead of taking another day off at home. She needed to rid herself of the chaos for a while.*

*Although, her family was her world, lately being around them made her feel like she was sinking into quicksand.*

*Janie welcomed her, "Good morning Miss. Hart. How are you today?" she hid her true answer behind a friendly smile and a pleasant reply.*

*"I'm good. Thank you." Jacquelyn sat at her desk, relishing the serenity in her office. Tilting her head back and closing her eyes, she said, "Why can't my home be like this?"*

*"Be like what?" she hadn't noticed Will's presence until now. He repeated his question as he came further into the office.*

*She answered, "Quiet, less disaster and more common sense."*

*"You know you wouldn't have it any other way. If it were different, you'd be bored," he said, smiling.*

*"I beg to differ. I could take a big heap of boredom right now," she said, throwing her head back on her chair.*

*"How are things at home?" asked Will.*

*"The window is being replaced today. One of Uncle Ray's buddies is doing the repair for free. That means no more money wasted on Deon's behalf. Everyone was out of the house by the time I got up, but enough about that, let's get started."*

*"Okay. I called the printer so he could make a few changes to the cover. We also have to finish the final preparations for the gala." Will went on about this and that as Jacquelyn visited la-la land. To seem as if she was giving him her full*

attention, Jacquelyn nodded her head and gave an occasional "I agree." Finally, Will caught on to her.

"Jacquelyn," he said, regaining her attention.

"What?" she said.

"You just agreed to catfish for lunch at Carol's diner," said Will.

"What's wrong with that?"

"You hate catfish, and you can't stand Carol's diner."

"Oh, maybe I didn't hear you correctly," said Jacquelyn.

"Or maybe you just weren't listening," said Will.

"No. I'm just tired. I couldn't sleep much last night," she said, rubbing her eyes.

"I'll go get lunch from the deli. You can take a nap on the couch in my office," offered Will.

"Sounds good," said Jacquelyn.

Janie came in saying, "Excuse me, Miss. Hart. You have a visitor."

"I didn't know that I had any appointments for the day," said Jacquelyn.

"His name is Deon," said Janie. Jacquelyn threw her hands up, saying, "There goes my nap. He's my brother, could you tell him to come in. Thanks, Janie."

"I'll be back with lunch," said Will leaving.

Deon came in. His demeanor had noticeably changed. His face had softened and was less stern.

"Hey. What brings you by?" asked a curious Jacquelyn.

"A lot," he said, sitting down.

"Such as?" said Jacquelyn clearly annoyed.

"I know you won't make this easy for me." He took in a deep breath and then went on. "I'm sorry."

"For?"

"You know, things have been crazy for a minute now. I let stuff get out of hand. I apologize for that, but you know what's going on in my life. I've been trying to balance everything. I haven't been doing the best job at that, though."

"Well, I really don't know what's going on with you these days. I mean getting arrested, people after you, you're barely around. Deon, this isn't you."

"Technically I wasn't arrested, I was taken in for questioning." He paused seeing that his sister's stance stiffened at his correction. "You're right," he said.

"You shut all of us out. We're entitled to our own lives and privacy. Still, there's a huge difference between privacy and secrecy," Jacquelyn got to the heart of the matter. "Why'd you push me away?"

"It wasn't completely on purpose. I needed to show myself that I could handle things without running to the family to *help me out. I get tired of running to mainly you and Uncle Ray like I can't handle myself. I'm not a kid Queen."*

*"That's what the family is supposed to be here for," said Jacquelyn.*

*"Yeah, but everyone gets to a point where they need to be independent. At the time, things were supposed to be simple. I was just a driver, like I said."*

*"But is that the only thing you did. Maybe I'm answering my own question. There's no way you'd be going through all of this if you were strictly sitting behind a wheel going from point A to point B," said an unconvinced Jacquelyn.*

*"It's not about what I did. It's more about what I know. I can't go into detail, but let's say I transported more than Fred and his friends around using Uncle Ray's cars. I needed money, period, and Ray's checks weren't enough. I wasn't involved in what Fred did, though. After I realized things were getting to deep and heard a few too many conversations I shouldn't have heard I quit. I thought Fred and I were still cool even when I wasn't his driver anymore. I messed up by taking Uncle Ray's limos and using them off the books as Fred's driver. I know I overstepped."*

*"Why was there so much urgency for the extra money?"*

*"Charlene needs to get to Cali more than you know, and so do I."*

*Jacquelyn didn't need to mention that their family could have provided him with the money. During that time frame, they were all struggling to make ends meet. She was at the boutique. Gwen and Ray had just moved in with Lena. Each of them had debts to settle. It's no wonder he ventured out on his own. Knowing Deon, he didn't want to be a burden.*

*"Why the sudden change with Fred, the window incident?"*

*"I guess they think I said something when I was taken in for questioning. I didn't give them anything against Fred, though," said Deon.*

*"Why not?" asked Jacquelyn.*

*"The police think that I know something about the arsons. I told them I don't and I have a real alibi. I was through with off-the-clock driving long before that happened. I know they're not done with me."*

*"What about the witness who saw you?"*

*Deon rolled his eyes. "They found their informant getting paid to lie about it by some of Fred's people. The only word they have to go from is Fred's."*

*"This is your future, Deon. You need to tell them what you know. Take whatever deal they're offering you if it comes to that."*

*"Things aren't that simple. Will's lawyer is working on the case for me. If I snitch, Fred can get somebody to hurt our family. If they do pen me for being connected with the whole*

*mess, I'm looking at a few years. I'd much rather take a sentence than have any of you taken away from me forever."*

*"What if you do take the deal?" asked Jacquelyn.*

*"That's being worked out right now. Either way, my hands are tied in some way. Queen, don't start. I got this."*

*"This is what you've chosen," she said hesitantly, then continued. "I have to respect that. Please be careful, Deon."*

*"I will. This is different," he said, now more relaxed.*

*"What?" Jacquelyn asked.*

*"The two of us are talking like adults without you acting like my momma. I like it."*

*"Me too," she said. Deon looked around his sister's office.*

*"I'm proud of you, not only for the job but... I just am."*

*"Thank you. That really means a lot."*

*"Well, maybe one day I'll give you a reason to say the same about me," said Deon.*

*"You have. A real man can admit when he's wrong without letting his pride get in the way."*

*"You don't have to say it because I said it," said Deon.*

*"Boy, I know that. I meant what I said."*

*"Okay. Well, let me get out of here. I need to recite the same speech to Uncle Ray and Grandma."*

*Jacquelyn laughed, "Alright, I'll see you at home."*

*This was the longest conversation in months. His visit was the most that she could ask for at that point. She wanted to believe that her brother had spoken from his heart, but Jacquelyn's instincts told her there was more to Deon's story.*

*Jacquelyn had tons of questions left to ask him. Instead of going forward with her miniature interrogation, she bit her tongue. The rest of her questions would have to be set aside. Jacquelyn was happy that her brother had opened up enough to begin to let her back into his life. Even though it was a fresh start, she knew their talk had not patched everything up. She couldn't fathom what repercussions awaited Deon while he was preparing for his future, which was sure to be completely altered. She had no clue how to play clean-up woman anymore. Was it even her place? Her relationship with him as his older sister wanted to protect and defend him through whatever he faced. Yet, the relationship she was beginning to evolve and she didn't want to risk losing him just because she felt indifferent.*

Chapter 12

*November 19, 1978 From the day I lost my daughter and her babies became mine my prayer has been to keep them safe and on the straight and narrow. I kept them in church, tried to steer them away from the riffraff, and made sure they kept their heads in their books. You just never know which you're your children will choose. You can pour all of yourself into them until you're empty, and it still feels like it's not enough. Queen told me about Deon. She wants to protect him from himself, but she's afraid that if she speaks out, he'll shut down on her again. If you ask me, a few crosswords can't break their bond. Those two stronger than either of them realize. Let it be if those words are what it takes to save him. Her love for her brother and her family has always been a tender spot. Even though Queen won't admit any of it, she thinks that if she tests their bond, she'll end up empty-handed. Love is constantly tested. If it is what it's supposed to be, love won't fade because of a few bumps or bruises in the relationship. I guess all of my babies have to find that out for themselves.*

*Jacquelyn remembered the anxiousness that she felt that evening. As a child, she loved roller coaster rides. The feeling that it gave her stomach as it approached the incline and then how the dip left her stomach was a distinct feeling she loved at one time. She had that same feeling as she prepared for the celebration of the gala event. Jacquelyn had not seen the anniversary gown since she bought it. She had purposely* placed it in the back of her closet. She would have gotten the butterfly feeling in her stomach if she had seen it each time she opened her closet. She wondered if she would even like her chosen dress. "What if it looks bad? What if I can't fit it anymore? I knew I should have gotten that black dress. Why did I listen to Aunt Gwen?" Those questions floated in Jacquelyn's head as she pulled through the clothes to get to her gown. She grabbed the hanger holding the gown, seeing that it was as pretty as she remembered it.

"Queen, you can worry about your dress later. Come sit down so I can finish your hair" said Gwen. Jacquelyn had popped up from the chair to match her dress with the right jewelry. That's the excuse she gave to her aunt. She needed to use that as an excuse to get away from the hot comb. Gwen could be dangerous with a hot comb, rolling iron, and the list goes on. Her hair sizzled from the heat then Jacquelyn screamed from a burn. Each time her niece yelled, Gwen would say, "Oh girl, that doesn't hurt". As she sat back down, she anticipated a burned scalp. "Fix your head right! You know I can't straighten your edges if you keep moving around," said Gwen fussing before continuing. "Girl, I swear the older you get, the more tender-headed you become."

"Maybe it wouldn't be as bad if you didn't put all that grease on my scalp. "Ouch!" groaned Jacquelyn."

"I barely touched your head. Anyway, I'm the one with the hot comb. Stay still. I'll be finished in a minute, "Jacquelyn *rolled her eyes instead of responding. "All done," said Gwen finishing the last piece of hair, "That wasn't too awful."*

*"You're not the one who was being tortured" said Jacquelyn patting her head.*

*"Like they say, beauty is pain. You're welcome."*

*"They weren't lying. A man must have come up with that phrase."*

*Deon happened to be walking past the room, overhearing them. "If that's the case, I never see you in any pain auntie."*

*Gwen threw a brush saying, "Keep it moving. I swear that boy is my payback for annoying your mama when we were kids." She looked around for the makeup. "Now it's time for the finishing touches."*

*"Oh, please don't make me look like a clown. You know I don't like colors that are too loud. Not too much blush, either. I don't want to look like I was playing in finger paint with Chris."*

*"Honey, I know what I'm doing. Who's the one that went to beauty school," said Gwen grabbing her makeup bag."*

*"Who's the one that didn't finish? You dropped out remember?"*

*"So? How much time have you spent in beauty school? Ha! I rest my case. Let an artist do her work" said Gwen kneeling down to Jacquelyn's face.*

*As long as that artist doesn't make me look like they work for Crayola, thought Jacquelyn. She patiently waited as her aunt applied the makeup to her face. Gwen dabbed the brush at the eye shadow, carefully choosing the perfect shade.*

*"Ooh, I've got the perfect lipstick for you" she said, digging into her bag. Gwen smoothed on the lipstick making sure she didn't smudge it. She finished her work and then said, "I'm done. Finally, this artist can put her tools away." She grabbed her various cosmetic applications, shoving them back into the bag. Taking a second look at Jacquelyn, she stopped what she was doing to say, "I am good. Don't look at yourself in the mirror until you have your dress and everything else on," Gwen placed a jacket over the mirror. "This way, you can't peek"*

*Jacquelyn looked the dress over again.*

*"I need some help with the zipper," said Jacquelyn struggling to zip herself into the dress. Gwen walked over to assist her. The zipper worked its way up without a hitch. Jacquelyn turned around to ask for her aunt's opinion. Before she could ask anything, Gwen spoke. "Absolutely beautiful. Wow, you look just like your mother. Let me go get Mama so she can see you." Jacquelyn saw her aunt tear up as she turned to walk away. Jacquelyn appreciated that compliment. Like most little girls, she wanted to look as beautiful as her mother. Growing up, Jacquelyn didn't think that she resembled her mother much. Only when she matured into a young woman*

did she see their resemblance. Lena came into the room teary-eyed herself.

"Look at my baby. You live up to your name," said Lena as she kissed her granddaughter's forehead. "My Queen is all grown up. Come to the front. Your Uncle Ray has his camera."

The threading was flawless. Her skin was highlighted by the gold in the dress. The gorgeous golden hues of her skin were further complemented by the cream color as the gown showcased her figure. Ray smiled from ear to ear as Jacquelyn posed for the camera.

"I feel like I'm getting ready for the prom all over again"" she said, laughing.

"I see Will's car pulling into the driveway. I'll bring him in here"" said Gwen. She walked Will into the living room to be involved in the pictures.

"Come on in, baby. You're included too. You look sharp in your suit." The pair posed as they said their goodbyes to Jacquelyn's family.

"Take care of our girl." said Ray from the doorway. The two of them were almost blinded by the flashes from the several cameras. When they sat in the car, they were finally able to speak to one another without interruptions like "Turn here" or "Move your head to the side"

"You look like an angel." he said sincerely."

"So do you." said Jacquelyn

He laughed and said, "I'll take that as you saying that I look nice."

"You look very handsome." said Jacquelyn

"Thank you, baby. Ready for tonight." said Will

"I should be asking you that. This is your big night." She held his hand, saying, "Your hand isn't sweating. I guess you're alright. I think I'm more nervous than you. Walking out of the house, I felt a little nauseous thinking about all those people. I'm glad I'm not the one giving a speech," she exhaled, "The last time I gave a speech was about four years ago. It was for my cousin's wedding. I was around my relatives, but even then, my knees buckled, and my voice squeaked. I made it through, though. You know what? That makes me feel better. The only thing I have to do is smile and clap for you." she said, looking at Will.

He looked at her and then said sarcastically, "Thanks for making me feel better about my speech that I have to give in front of hundreds of my colleagues".

"Oh, I didn't mean to say it like that. You give great speeches. You're used to speaking in front of a crowd. There's no need for you to be nervous." She glanced at Will, who was starting to look nervous. She saw tiny beads of sweat forming on his *head. She tried to encourage him. "Do you want to practice it?"*

*"I think I'll be fine," he said, smiling at her. As they approached the building where the party was being held Jacquelyn's nerves loosened. She gazed at the grand structure. There were endless rows of cars, indicating the vast number of people gathered there.*

*"Looks like a full house. More people to cheer you on," she said, reassuring him.*

*The valet drove the car away as Will and Jacquelyn entered the ballroom arm and arm. The room was decorated with past covers of Empire. The covers dated back to the very first issue of the magazine. Will had big shoes to feel, which he already knew. He looked proud as they made their way to their designated table. His parents were already seated as they greeted the couple. His mother was dressed stunningly from head to toe, as was his father. Both of the couples were breathtaking. Soon enough, the time came for Will to give his speech. Jacquelyn could see he was initially nervous, but as he continued, he began to display why his father entrusted him with his company.*

*"I have incredible shoes to fill, but I intend on doing so. My father's legacy stretches well beyond a few magazine pages. I hope to continue carrying on his title not for his namesake but to make a difference in ways such as he has. The community helped shape the man my father is today, and in return, my father helps shape the community. Through integrity and hard work, Empire will continue to thrive." Jacquelyn watched as the partygoers listened to Will. Even*

*the ladies from the "Hen House" seemed attentive to what he was saying. Janie gazed at him like a proud mother.*

*Mrs. Jacobs whispered to her husband, "Doesn't he remind you of when he used to give his Easter speeches." They beamed as they enjoyed their son's speech. Finally, he came to an ending.*

*"On behalf of Jacobs Publishing, I would like to thank everyone for coming out to celebrate with us in honoring both of my parents and those involved from past through present." Mr. Jacobs was the first to stand to his feet applauding. After Will left the podium, he excused himself and Jacquelyn.*

*"We'll be right back" he explained.*

*"Is everything okay?" asked a concerned Jacquelyn. "If you're worried about how you did, you shouldn't. You were amazing" she said sincerely."*

*"That's not it. I just wanted to show you something." She assumed he wanted to show her a gift for his parents. They walked off the elevator, and she became increasingly doubtful about her assumption. Will sped up his pace while she tried to keep up with him. High heels and a lengthy dress aren't ideal for a sprint. He slowed down and then came to a halt when they came to an empty ballroom. It was lit with hundreds of candles." He walked her to the opposite end of the room. A huge window framed the perfect view of the city.*

*He had allowed her to put his image, name, and hard work in her hands. In his parents' circle, the image was one of a person's most valued assets. At her most vulnerable states, his trust never wavered. Her revelation of his devotion came to her at a perfect time. She looked over at Will, who was already staring at her.*

*"What is all of this?" He pulled her closer, saying, "You can see our building from here." Jacquelyn's eyes went from admiring the stunning architecture of the structure to spotting unusual motions on the roof. "Hey do you see that?" she asked, pointing to the building. Will took notice looking in the direction as well. "No one's supposed to be up there. Do you think we should call the police or have security check it out?"*

*Strangely Will kept his relaxed demeanor, saying, "Wait. Look closer," he told her. Jacquelyn saw two figures moving something around, coming closer to the roof's edge. The two individuals draped a large banner over the side of the building. She read the sign slowly aloud while straining to read the words. "Jacquelyn Hart, Will you marry me?" Will was already down on one knee when she finished reading the sign. Every thought in her head disappeared. She was quickly brought back to reality when the street light's glare bounced off the diamond gleaming in her eyes. Her response made up for the delay.*

*"Yes!" she said, almost knocking him and the ring to the floor. He laughed at her excitement. The guests at the party had their own excitement as they discovered the sign and loudly cheered below. He didn't want to make a production out of their engagement because he knew his bride to be hated the attention. He wanted that moment to belong to the two of them, at least for the night.*

*"We can celebrate the good news with my parents tomorrow. I know my mother and she'll be ready to jump into planning*

the engagement party ASAP," he said as they drove away. He took her to the restaurant where they had their first date. After they enjoyed their meals and the old memories that they had shared, he took her home. Jacquelyn expected the house to be quiet and for everyone to be resting. Everything in the house was quiet, but everyone was not resting. All the ladies of the house were seated at the kitchen table sipping tea. One spot had an empty cup waiting for Jacquelyn.

"You two didn't have to wait up for me"" she said modestly.

"Oh no, we wanted to make sure the future Mrs. Jacobs made it in safely." said Gwen grinning.

"How did you find out?" said Jacquelyn while she sat beside her grandmother.

"You know he has to get the family's blessing first. He came to speak to Momma and your Uncle Ray a few weeks ago. They were too excited to keep it to themselves." said Gwen "I'm surprised you could keep it quiet this long." said Jacquelyn.

Gwen reached for Jacquelyn's hand, "Let me see that ring, honey!" The ladies gushed over the exquisite ring.

"I have a big wedding to plan" said Lena, "Soon, this house will be empty." she said with a slight hint of sadness. She changed the subject, not wanting to bring down their night. "I remember when your Daddy proposed. We had been courting for two years. Even after I had moved during those two years with my family, we kept up through letters. When I came back to visit family, he made sure he saw me. He asked me to marry him two weeks after I arrived in town. He wrote me a letter for all of our anniversaries. I kept every one of them."

"I remember my engagement too. Ray hasn't always been the romantic type. I had just finished my shift at Burgers-n-Buns. My feet were swollen, and I smelt like grease. He proposed on the porch with a bundle of Mama's roses. He was too broke to buy some from a florist." said Gwen smacking her lips.

"I think that it was sweet. He gave you what he could. It's the thought that counts." said Jacquelyn.

"He should have thought harder." said Gwen.

"I agree with Queen. Be grateful that you have a man who wants to be around you for the rest of his life especially with that sassy attitude." said Lena.

"I guess so. He never complained about my sassy attitude back then. He learned about Mama and Daddy's letters. He wanted to give me something to remember, so he gave me a bundle of roses on our wedding anniversaries. On our first wedding anniversary, he filled the house with roses to make up for the ones he couldn't get when he proposed."

Amid their joy, they heard abrupt banging on the door. The banging on the door grew louder and more demanding.

"Who could be at the door this time of night?" said Lena as she stood up to answer the unexpected visitor. Lena grabbed the bat behind the door.

"If it's the police for Deon, I'm turning him in!" yelled Gwen jokingly. Lena ignored her remark as she cautiously looked through the peephole.

"I don't believe it," said Lena as she began to undo the multiple locks and resting the bat on the floor. Each time Lena heard of a break-in, she added another lock. She would have installed steel bars, but everyone else in the house complained that it already felt like a prison without them. They dealt with the locks for Lena's comfort. She opened the door to reveal a pitiful-looking Mr. Brown. His shoulders were slumped over, his eyes were red, and he reeked of cheap alcohol and cigarettes. He mumbled a few words to Lena as Gwen and Jacquelyn listened to his inaudible whispers. Lena led him to the kitchen table. The ladies greeted him as he sat down and managed to say "Good evening". He pulled a wrinkled piece of paper from his coat pocket. His random visit had to have something to do with what was in the letter that now rested in the middle of the table. Mr. Brown let out an exasperated sigh before telling them the reason for his awkward presence.

"I found this letter in my mailbox today. She finally turned out to be everything I tried to keep her from becoming. She left me just like her momma. She went to that woman's wretched family." he said, speaking through his teeth.

"Are you saying Charlene's in California? I just saw her earlier today," said a shocked Jacquelyn.

"Go check her room," said Lena.

Mr. Brown turned his attention to Jacquelyn. "How'd you know Charlene would be California?"

Before Mr. Brown question Jacquelyn any further, Gwen announced, "She's gone!" Ray and Deon entered the house, and the focus was now placed on Deon. Mr. Brown pushed past everyone, his big belly leading the way.

"You're the one who started up this mess. I could just wring your neck." he said, lunging forward toward Deon.

"If you even think about touching my boy, Charlene won't be the only one missing," threatened Lena. Mr. Brown stopped, almost frozen by her words. He was surprised that this kind of reaction came from her. Lena was usually the calm one no matter what the situation was. "This has gone way too far. Your daughter's heart was shut off from you long before she left your home. If it wasn't for my grandson, she probably would've lost her mind over there with you. The truth is hard to face, but it's about time you look it straight in the eye. We're going to figure this out. Now sit down!" Mr. Brown, along with the rest of the family, remained motionless. Lena looked around, "People, I didn't say all of that for my health. Sit down now!" Everyone complied. Whether they were at the dinner table or sofa, each behind was swiftly seated. "I think the best thing you can do for your daughter right now is to leave her alone. Deon, I'm sure you know exactly where

*Charlene is. Ask her to call her father, do something to let him know she's okay."*

*His eyes failed to meet his grandmother's, but Deon gave a quick, "Yes, ma'am."*

Chapter 13

*The months that followed were filled with confusion, relief, and bittersweet moments. Admid the joy of her engagement, Jacquelyn continued to ponder about Charlene's absence. She could not quite understand how her friend could be so committed to Deon one day and abandon him the next. As far as she was concerned, Charlene was the main reason Deon had gotten trapped in the entire web of lies that Fred had created. Lena, however, was not into passing the blame. She argued that Deon was no longer a child. She and Jacquelyn could no longer cover the dirty tracks he had created. Although she would stand by her grandson, she would not allow Charlene to be a scapegoat for his actions. Lena sympathized with Charlene's desire to find her lost bond with her mother, and if that meant leaving, then so be it. Jacquelyn was not easily swayed by the emotional history behind Charlene's departure, but she kept her opinion to herself when Deon was around. For whatever reason, her brother was at peace with Charlene's decision. He told his sister she'd soon understand.*

*Jacquelyn's temper would shortly be idled. Jacquelyn came home to find her grandmother cleaning the house from top to bottom. "No, the flowers should be here. No, there," said Gwen. She took pleasure in directing the others. Deon's involvement with the case of Fred was coming to an end. The only time Lena cleaned like this was for company or when she was too upset to talk. Everyone seemed to be on their best behavior lately, so she assumed they'd soon be expecting guests.*

*"Who's all of this for?" asked Jacquelyn as she coughed from the heavy scent of furniture polish.*

*"Someone I know you've just been dying to see," said Gwen as she passed Jacquelyn a postcard. She read Charlene's name at the top of the card and didn't need to read any further as she quickly passed it back to her Aunt. The two experienced many battles, with Lena always on Charlene's defense.*

*"So she runs off, and then we automatically welcome her back with open arms?" said Jacquelyn as she followed her grandmother into the kitchen.*

*Lena turned to face her granddaughter, "If your brother wanted our approval, he would've come to us, but he's made it clear that he doesn't. The only opinion that matters regarding this subject is Deon's, and he understands. Why can't you?"*

*Jacquelyn threw her hands up, saying, "It makes no sense."*

*"Weak argument, Queen," yelled Gwen from the front room.*

*"She had the right to rebuild a relationship that was broken. You ought to understand that out of all people. You know what it's like not to have your mother. She can't change the mess that her parents made for her. Don't blame her for forgiving her mother and offering her a second chance," said Lena.*

*"What about the mess that she helped Deon make? He purposely involved himself with a criminal all to give her mother a second chance she really doesn't deserve. We all stood by and watched Mr. Brown botch what was left of*

*Charlene's childhood when her mama left. It's like a domino effect and the next heart break in line is my brother's."*

*"Nothing's broken!" said Lena slamming the drawer. "And if you don't learn how to forgive and let your brother grow up you will be the only one with broken heart." She had lost her patience and the desire to continue the conversation. Luckily Lena did not have to proceed in this redundant debate with Jacquelyn. They heard car doors shutting and voices approaching the porch.*

*"That's them. Now I won't ask you to behave because you're not a child, but I will ask you to be respectful," said Lena patting Jacquelyn's arm. Jacquelyn knew her grandmother never asked for much, so she could hold her tongue and be polite for at least a night or two.*

*Ray walked in carrying a large suitcase. "Look who we found," he said while placing the luggage beside him. Ray stepped aside to make room for their guest to enter. Jacquelyn hadn't seen Mrs. Brown since childhood but could never forget her face. Jacquelyn saw her face in Charlene's whenever she smiled. Mrs. Brown, known for her long dark brown hair, now had a head full of grey, and a short haircut framed her face.*

*"Carol, it's been so long," said Lena embracing her old friend. She spotted Jacquelyn and stretched her arms, saying, "Oh, my God. That can't be Queen. Give me a hug." Mrs. Brown made her way across the room. "Spitting image of your mother," said Mrs. Brow as she made her way across the room. "The last time I saw you, well, you were in pigtails, and*

you didn't have those," she said, pointing at Jacquelyn's chest.

"Well, a lot has changed," said a blushing Jacquelyn.

Shallow chatter began as Jacquelyn's curiosity about Charlene tugged away at her. If she wanted to be a part of their family so much, what's taking her so long to come in? Then, just as her irritation mounted, she saw Charlene walking through the doorway. Her face was fuller, and she looked more like a woman than a young girl. She seemed to have lost the dark shadow that had followed her for so long. California's sunshine had given her a glow all her own. Jacquelyn felt herself smiling. Underneath her ill feelings, Jacquelyn really did miss her friend.

"Hi, everyone," said Charlene in her shy voice. Lena was the first to approach her, quickly embracing her in her arms. Deon eased in, carrying a bundle in his arms as the two shared words. Jacquelyn's was nearly taken away when she saw a small hand slip from underneath the blanket.

Gwen didn't miss a beat as she swiftly took notice, "Carol, I know that's not your baby?" The room grew silent as they waited for Mrs. Brown to react.

"Not exactly," she responded. Charlene moved to Deon's side, and Gwen and everyone else received their answer. Charlene's absence and Deon's uncharacteristic reaction now made sense to Jacquelyn. It was no wonder that with Deon's life's chaos, he wouldn't want Charlene or their child anywhere near. Yet, as the understanding set in, so did the guilt of judging her once close friend.

"We'd like to introduce someone to you all," said Deon as he uncovered the sleeping infant. Watching her grandmother's demeanor, Jacquelyn knew that this new edition was not a surprise to her. Lena had to have known the entire time leading her to defend Charlene's decision. "Oh." was the only thing Gwen could say as she took a big gulp of her drink.

Deon placed the baby in his grandmother's arms. Chris moved forward to get a better view of his new cousin.

"We wanted to include both sides of the family. Her name is Victoria, after Deon's mother and we call her Tori for short," said Charlene.

"I love it. Hello Vitoria Hart," said Gwen kissing the infant's cheek. "Wow, this is my great niece. I can't wait to spoil her. My sister would be so happy."

"Yes. She would be thrilled about her first grandchild," said Lena."

"Awe. I want another one," said Gwen. Everyone was surprised, but no one was nearly as surprised as Ray. He gasped at her statement.

"What did she say?" he asked as if he hadn't heard his wife.

"What you heard," said Gwen responding in a cooing voice while gazing at the baby. Ray scratched his head before speaking.

"Uh, I think you've been inhaling too much baby powder. Gwen pass that baby to Jacquelyn." She rolled her eyes and slowly passed Victoria to Jacquelyn.

"I'm almost afraid to hold her. She's so small." Jacquelyn held her niece, almost afraid to breathe or move. She felt like the slightest movement would break her.

"Queen, you don't have to be stiff. She won't fall to pieces. Just support her neck and her head. You're doing fine," said Lena. After getting comfortable holding her niece, Jacquelyn understood how her Aunt felt. She didn't want to part with her either. Finally, she let go long enough for her *grandmother to hold her. "You are as pretty as your mother and your grandmothers. I think that's a smile," said Lena relishing in the moment of holding her first great-grandchild. With Tori at home in those first few hours everything was right in their world. For that short time, debts were erased, busted windows had never happened, and impending trials didn't exist. The shock of Deon being a father dissipated as the family clamored around the baby.*

*On her way back to her room Jacquelyn saw her brother standing outside of his old room which now served as a makeshift the nursery, watching Charlene and their child sleep. "Looking at her makes you think there's not a care in the world," said Jacquelyn.*

*"I wish it really was that way. I actually forgot about everything else that's been going on," said Deon.*

*"I hate to bring it up, but have you heard from your lawyers about Fred's trial?"*

*"I've done my part, and I'll be testifying. Then I'm done," he said in a solemn tone.*

*"Then why don't you sound happy about it? You'll have your family, peace of mind and your freedom."*

*"Yeah, but at what cost? Fred isn't the type of man to just let things go. Damned if you do, damned if you don't, I guess."*

*"You're doing what you have to do. I think you should feel good about that. You will always be my mother's child. Because of this my need to protect you will always be there, but now I see that you have your own family to protect so I have to loosen those reigns a bit. Hurts a little to let go, but after watching you today what choice do I have? I'm proud of*

*you for doing all of the things necessary to take care of Charlene and your little girl."*

*Even though he had his own family to look after, her obligation to him hadn't declined. Her commitment may have been interpreted as overbearing occasionally, but Deon always knew she meant well. "I also need to do what I have to do and apologize to you about the way I was towards Charlene. Even though I didn't know the whole story, I should've known that the person I've known all of those years wouldn't abandon you. I just thought..."*

*Deon cut her short, saying, "Apology accepted."*

*"What? I wasn't finished, though," said Jacquelyn*

*"I know this isn't that easy for you. Usually, I'm on the other side doing the apologizing."*

*"Whoa. You really are growing up. A few months ago, if we had this same conversation, you'd really be enjoying hearing me ask for forgiveness," she said, stunned.*

*"I don't have much of a choice," he said, glancing in on his daughter.*

*The next day Jacquelyn went to work bright and early. She had taken a few days off to help prepare the house for Charlene and Tori. The last day that she was there was before the anniversary dinner. No one outside her family knew about her and Will's engagement. She tried to speed walk past the "Hen House." She successfully moved through without being noticed. However, the elevator didn't have an escape route. Nadine, one of the top "Hens", happened to be getting on the elevator at the same time as Jacquelyn. She was known around the office as a fast talker. Her words came out in a rush, jumbling together, and she clamored at the slightest hint of gossip.*

*"Hi Jacquelyn, I haven't seen you in a while. How've you been?" She didn't give her a chance to answer. "That's good. By the way, I loved your dress at the gala. You left early, though. I stayed the entire night. Everybody talked about what a mess Shelly was. Claudia who works in accounting found out that she and Drew, the photographer, have been having an affair. Everybody knew...except his wife who happens to be Claudia's friend. The wife mysteriously found out during the gala" Nadine looked down, spotting Jacquelyn's ring. "Oh my! What is that on your finger, girl?" she said, snatching Jacquelyn's hand. "You and Mr. Jacobs...ooh, I gotta tell—I mean inform the other ladies. We can throw you an engagement party!"*

*Fortunately, they had arrived on Jacquelyn's floor. She was always good about taking off her ring before she came to the office. Unfortunately, her niece had colic. Her tiny cry grew louder each night, and the lack of sleep had won the battle over Jacquelyn's memory. She didn't even give the elevator a chance to fully open before dashing out. She swiftly left Nadine and her chatter behind without even attempting to explain or accept her congratulations. She made a beeline to*

Will's office. Jacquelyn walked in as he was ending a phone conversation. Jacquelyn shut the door and took a seat.

"Thank you, sir; we'll be in touch," he said with his business voice. He then directed his attention to his fiancé. "Hey, stranger."

"Hey, boss, I think we need to announce our engagement sooner than we had planned," she said, shaking her head.

"I thought we were going to enjoy the privacy before letting my parents hijack our engagement because we know once the office finds out it's going to spread like wildfire and my parents love a big spectacle. I thought we agreed to wait after they returned from their trip. Why the sudden change in plans?" he asked, sitting forward.

"Nadine ran into me on the way up. She has eyes like a hawk that keep up with her fast mouth. She saw the ring. I'd estimate that the first two floors knew about three minutes ago."

"Okay, baby, no stress. We can call my parents today and the circus may begin." Jacquelyn would have liked to have gone with their initial plans, but she knew the freedom of enjoying their engagement privately was fleeting from the beginning. It was nice to have something to themselves just for a few short lived moths. From the day that Jacquelyn walked through the doors of the Jacobs' building she was the hot topic of discussion. The boss's girlfriend so of course she gets a nice office. Of course she gets the best projects at work. Her family is from the rough side of the tracks, her brother is a criminal, but of course Mr. Jacobs is going to take care of it.

*Criticism was nothing new, yet, it was nice to excluded for the time being.*

*"We need to get Nadine a muzzle for Christmas," said Will, who was more humored than upset.*

*Jacquelyn exhaled and settled into her chair.*

*"Why are you so tense?" he asked after observing Jacquelyn.*

*"You know how things have been lately. It was hard for me to imagine things going smoothly with everything else going on," said Jacquelyn.*

*"Things seem to be looking up, though."*

*"In some ways, they are. I mean, I have an adorable niece. She looks like me."*

*"That's Gwen kicking in again," said Will jokingly.*

*"I can't help that the baby shares my good genes," she grinned.*

*"I bet everyone in the house is claiming the same thing."*

*"Yes," she said, laughing. "She's one of the few positive highlights."*

*"What's another?" he asked.*

*"Us, but you already knew that. You just wanted to hear me say it."*

*"Yeah, you caught me," he said, holding her hand as he sat on the edge of his desk.*

*"And then there's Deon," she said as her tone dropped and her smile melted away. "He's supposed to enjoy having Charlene and his baby here, but he just won't allow himself. I guess, in his mind, it's too good to be true. I know he did the*

*right thing by testifying against Fred. If he hadn't cooperated, who knows where he'd be." Deon had intended to use his side cash flow as a means of stability for his family. Although in Jacquelyn's point of view his purpose was pure-hearted, his deeds must be thoroughly thought through. Unfortunately, his good intentions were overshadowed by his flawed actions. Deon, as well as his family, had been anticipating the trial. Fred Thomas had several charges against him. Deon's testimony was vital to the prosecutor's advantage. Newspapers had a field day heightening the drama. Jacob's publishing chose to stay away from the story or any others relating to it for Jacquelyn's sake. Her brother's testimony added another flaw to Fred's defense. Fred took his former acquaintance's disloyalty personal. As Deon spoke, everyone noticed the defenses' eyes grow cold. Deon realized that each word that he revealed were shots against him. Fred had never confessed to working with Deon. He only admitted to having a business tie with the young man. The police used Deon's fears of his former accomplice turning on him. The authorities used this to pull evidence that would've otherwise stayed unknown. After learning the truth during the trial, he was convinced that Mr. Thomas would strike back.*

*He tried to keep his mind clear of the concerns in front of his family, but they knew it was taking its toll on him. Some nights he woke up drenched in sweat with his heart pounding. Jacquelyn was the only one who knew of his late-night disturbances because her room was right next to his. She'd hear him talking loudly in his sleep and then woke him up. He'd look up at her confused, then comforted that* she was there. Jacquelyn asked a couple of times what the dreams were about, and he always said that he didn't remember. She saw through his facade. It must have been too terrible to share. She didn't pressure him to tell her about his dreams. Jacquelyn just told him that it would be okay. Those few words gave him many peaceful nights of sleep as a child. She didn't even have to know the circumstances or details. These days, however, he knew that his sister couldn't protect him from the inevitable forever. Back then, he was afraid of being alone in the dark. He grew out of it later, forgetting about his nightlight. Presently his sister served the purpose. Yet, even on the brightest days, he couldn't shake his fears of what would come. Lately, his boogieman went by several names, but the most current name was Fred Thomas.

*Chapter 14*

*December 8, 1978 Dear Diary, Don't let your stepping stones become your stumbling blocks." That's a phrase I heard from my parents throughout my life. I only understood it later when I had already done so. Too many times I'd let things, that should have been a simple trip me up. Deon is dealing with his own blocks. His mistakes have become both a blessing and a curse. I'm grateful for our baby girl Victoria. Initially, things were a little shaky, but Deon has become an incredible man, and I'm thankful for Charlene's presence in his life. Yet, there are those other things, like his guilt about running around with this Fred character. We all stumble, but it's up to him to decide what to do in his struggle. If I know him well enough, he'll do what needs to be done.*

*Before anything else damaged the good things going on, Deon wanted to settle more critical parts of his life. That's when the rest of the family fell into place. Jacquelyn informed Will of their plans.*

*"Okay, if you could be here by three that would be perfect. I'm supposed to be Charlene's distraction. Her father and a couple other guests should be here when you arrive," she*

*spoke up, trying to compete with her niece's loud crying in the background.*

*"Sounds like the baby is competing with Gwen to be the loudest mouth in the family," said Will.*

*"Yeah, she's definitely a Hart. Gwen and Tori are both keeping up a bunch of noise. Charlene is trying to put Tori down for her nap, and Gwen is taking her party-planning duty to the head. As usual, she's bossing everyone around." She left the hallway and went to her room to escape the noise. "Can you hear me better now? Good."*

*"Does Charlene suspect anything?" he asked.*

*"As far as I know, she just thinks that we're throwing my engagement party." With all of the decorations, it was the perfect cover-up. The entire family was helping Deon prepare his wedding to Charlene right under her nose. Gwen was going to alert Jacquelyn to get the bride to be out of the house. While Jacquelyn provided the distraction, the rest of the family welcomed the minister and the rest of the guests.*

They even had a dress already tucked away for her. Gwen came into her room, interrupting her conversation.

"Queen, get with it. You're the biggest part of this. Come on, honey," she said, pulling her by the arm like she would do her son.

"Alright, see you at three," said Jacquelyn as she was pulled away from the phone. "Gwen, that's so rude," she said with her hands on her hips.

"Well, I'm sorry, but rude or not, we have to get this show on the road. Now you know your part in this, right?"

"Yeah, yeah, you went over it a thousand times. I'm not a kid. I understand simple instructions." She glanced at the time before going on. "Before I go, I want to check on Deon.

"Apparently, you don't understand simple instructions. Girl, make it quick," said Gwen with a hostile voice. "Sure," she said, waving her hand toward her aunt. Jacquelyn would handle things as quickly or slowly as she wanted, regardless of Gwen's or anyone else's plans. She opened the door to find her brother pacing back and forth.

"Cold feet?" she asked. He looked like the typical groom nervously contemplating his impending vows.

"Why do you say that?" he asked, stammering.

"You're about to wear a hole in Grandma's rug. Just relax," she said as she picked up his necktie from his chair. "You haven't even finished getting ready. Let me help you out," she said, adjusting his tie.

"Do you think I'm doing the right thing? What if it doesn't work?" implored Deon.

"If you had asked me this last year, I probably would have laughed, and then I would've answered no. But since this isn't last year and none of us are the same, my answer is yes. I think you are more than ready to take on family life. I never thought my baby brother would be getting married before me."

"Neither did I," he said, laughing.

"Knock, knock. I'm not rushing you two am I Queen?" asked Gwen.

"Enough with the sarcasm, I'm ready. You're ready, too," said Jacquelyn smiling at her brother.

"Now, get Charlene out of here. The photographer is on his way. By the time you get back, everything should be set."

Jacquelyn approached Charlene, who looked exhausted after finally getting her baby girl to sleep. She didn't want to disturb her, but she didn't want to mess up the plan. "Hey, would you mind running a quick errand with me?"

"I don't mind. Actually, it would be nice to get out of the house. I don't think I've been past the mailbox since we brought the baby home." Chris saw them headed for the door and immediately grabbed his jacket.

"Queen, I wanna go too," he said, holding on to his cousin.

"Just let him go," said Ray.

Chris had a sugar high from all the cookies Lena had hidden in the pantry. No one knew he had gotten into them until they saw him running around the house and jumping on the beds. Not even the threat of a spanking calmed him down.

"I am. He knows I can't resist that face anyway," said Jacquelyn holding his hand. She waited a few minutes for the car to warm up before taking off. They passed Charlene's old home and saw her father walking down his driveway.

"Why is my father dressed up? I know he's not going for a walk in that suit," she said, pointing towards Mr. Brown. He had forgiven himself and his daughter, and she granted him acceptance in return.

"Maybe he has a date," said Jacquelyn.

"I doubt it, but who knows, right?"

"Right," agreed Jacquelyn.

"So where are we headed to?" asked Charlene.

"To Sugar's bakery, I have to pick up the cake for the party." The only thing that Chris heard from them was cake.

"Ooh, I want cake," he shouted over their chatter.

"I promised him a special slice," said Jacquelyn as she parked in front of the bakery. "Alright, Chris, keep Charlene company quietly, and you'll still get some cake."

"We'll be fine," said Charlene.

Jacquelyn and Mario, the store's manager, made small talk as they brought the rest of the cakes to the front. He was the first to notice the black car driving around the parking lot. The car had sped around the bakery twice before slowing down but not coming to a complete stop. The passenger in the back seat rolled the window down just enough to do what they had come for. The first shot came straight through the bakery's window, shattering the glass.

"Get down!" yelled Mario.

The other workers dropped their boxes and hit the floor as Mario jumped over the counter to shield Jacquelyn. Shots flared and rang in their ears as they sought protection. What seemed like hours had only taken place in a matter of seconds. Shattered glass and busted boxes of cake and frosting covered the ground. The gunshots had stopped, but *their ears had been pierced by the sound. Mario made sure everyone was unharmed.*

*"Is everyone okay?" he asked.*

*The handful of customers and employees were quick to respond. Jacquelyn shook fragments of glass off of her jacket. She gained her senses, remembering her family was still in the car.*

*"Oh Jesus," she said, jumping to her feet.*

*"Wait!" ordered Mario.*

*Ignoring his order, she darted out of the building. Caution was the last thing on her mind. She slid on the ice on the sidewalk as she made her way to the passenger side. Her body trembled as she swung open the back door. She found Chris covering his ears and shaking on the car's floor. She grabbed him and held him in her arms.*

*"I want mama?" he cried, hiding his face in his cousin's chest.*

*"I know baby. It's okay they're gone. Charlene, it's okay to get up now it's over." Her friend remained silent. The deafening silence sent chills through her body. "I want you to stay right here," she instructed her cousin.*

*"No!" he cried, holding on to Jacquelyn tightly.*

*He refused to let go, so she carried him to the other side of the vehicle with her. Mario ran up to her, and she asked him to hold Chris while she checked on her friend. Jacquelyn opened the door to see Charlene slumped over across the seat. Blood from her body stained the cushions and had splattered onto the dashboard. Jacquelyn's scream from the sight* echoed. She held her friend in her arms, trying to shake her back to consciousness.

"It's okay; you can wake up now. Please!" she kept begging as her voice shrieked. Jacquelyn rocked her back and forth, kneeling down on her knees. No matter how much she begged, Charlene's body remained motionless. Mario held Chris protectively. He studied the block, maybe hoping to spot the car, but the shooters had sped away. Jacquelyn listened to the deafening silence as she waited to hear at least one breath from Charlene's motionless body. They'd escaped leaving ruin and taking with them Charlene's life. The damage that they had caused would stretch beyond that afternoon.

The police arrived, and the witnesses, including Jacquelyn, followed the routine that went with it. Then, she faced the reality of returning home and delivering the message. Jacquelyn pondered how one relays the news that someone's daughter, mother, or fiancée has been robbed of their most precious gift. Jacquelyn knew that Charlene was gone before the car's wheels screeched away. Perhaps that's why she didn't check on her first. She knew her friend was gone before she opened the car door.

The loss of her parents felt as fresh as Charlene's blood that now stained Jacquelyn's clothes. It had been sixteen years since she and Deon had lost their parents. From the time that she had lost them, she felt cheated. Although she was now an adult, she missed the luxury of knowing they were there. Sometimes Jacquelyn would lapse into daydreams about them. She'd think about how she would visit them on weekends and go shopping with her mother. They would have *late-night talks and laugh when they remembered funny moments. One of the things Jacquelyn resented the most was that she would never be able to sit and talk to her mother as a grown woman. She would never know what her mother thought of her first boyfriend, or watch her face light up to seeing Jacquelyn dressed up for her graduation. Her father would never walk her down the aisle. She couldn't reminisce on things that she did as a child with her parents. Those times were lost to her memory and could only be refreshed through her mother's or father's words.*

*She now pondered upon the easiest way to break the news to her family without breaking down herself. Nothing about what she had to do would be easy. No matter how delicately a person placed the words on their tongue, by the time they fell from their lips on the other person's ears, it always sounded as ugly as it indeed was. She recalled the way her Grandfather told her about her parents' deaths. He took Jacquelyn and her brother out for popcorn and then to the park. He attempted to find the easiest way to make them understand it. Not only had his grandchildren lost their parents, but he had also lost his daughter. When he finally did tell them, Jacquelyn ran away, dropping her popcorn. Her Grandfather caught up with her and tried to comfort her. She cried every day and could remember her eyes being red for almost a month. Well into her late teens, she gagged at the smell of popcorn. Deon was too young to realize what everything meant. When he finally realized what it meant and that his parents weren't coming home, his cries for Mommy and Daddy followed.*

*A police officer offered to drive her and Chris home. On the eight-minute drive home, she collected her thoughts and pulled herself together as best she could. She told herself she couldn't cry because she had to remain strong for the others. Chris didn't even question her about why Charlene wasn't with them. She assumed he knew what had happened. Gwen would have to bear the burden of introducing her son to something that went hand in hand with life.*

*"Is this your stop, miss?" asked the officer.*

*"Yes sir, thank you," she replied. She asked the officer not to park directly in front of the house, she didn't want to alarm them with the sight of the cop car. Indeed the family had to suspect that something was wrong. Unfortunately, Jacquelyn had to confirm their fears. Her feet weighed her down like lead as she approached the house. The door opened, and thankfully it wasn't Deon.*

*"Hey girl, I thought we were gonna have to send a search party out for you. Where's Charlene? Don't tell me we have a runaway bride," said Ray. His jokes ceased once he saw his niece and son's faces. He glanced at the policeman's car creeping away. That's when he noticed his niece's disheveled appearance. "Queen, what's happened? Where's the car?" His mind searched for the worst, and Jacquelyn's eyes spoke for her. Chris ran to his mother immediately when she stepped*

outside with them. "Baby girl, just tell me," he begged, holding her niece's hand.

"I was—I was inside of the bakery, and Charlene and Chris were waiting for me in the car. It only took a minute, but a car drove by and fired shots. By the time I made it to the car...she was gone." Tears broke through and Jacquelyn's voice cracked. She choked on the last sentence barely getting the words out.

Gwen's jaws dropped in shock. Each word was a struggle as she felt her heart sink with each one. "Oh God," was the only thing that her aunt could get out. Ray hung his head down, covering his eyes to hide the tears. Jacquelyn embraced her aunt, making an effort to console her. After a few minutes, they decided to inform the others what had happened. They thought it would be best to tell Deon, Lena, and Mr. Brown together, aside from the guests. They whisked them to the back room for more privacy. When Ray recited Jacquelyn's story Mr. Brown faded into a man whose spirit had been broken.

He cried out, "This was supposed to be the beginning. This can't be it."

He repeated his words over and over to Lena while she cried. Deon stood there with his feet firmly planted on the ground. He took in everything that had been said. Jacquelyn watched as her brother stood before her, devastated. She tried to hug him, but he angrily yelled, "No! No! It's not true!" His fists were clenched as he punched the wall again and again. He hurried out of the room, not wanting to deal with the truth.

She chased after him saying,

"Deon, wait, please. I know you don't want to hear it, but..."

"But what? Look at what you're telling me! I can't accept that!" he yelled as he jumped into his car, slamming the car door behind him. By then, the wedding guests had overheard them and were leaving. They assumed that the family would like time to themselves.

Chapter 15

*Dear Diary, Sometimes the beginning really is the end. I know life doesn't provide us with the answers that we always want. I pray that my grandson can understand the slightest hints of why things have happened without being struck with guilt and blame for the rest of his life. I pray that this too shall pass. This has had far too many losses. I don't know how we can make it through yet another. Another child has lost their mother.*

*Before the caution-taped area was presumed, it was clear that Fred Thomas was the force behind the devastation. When the first bullet shell hit the ground, his revenge had begun. It wouldn't resonate until Victoria was old enough to know what that day had taken and the heartache it had added. That's when his vengeance would come full circle. Charlene's case was wrapped up fairly quickly, and it didn't take the community long to help put the pieces together. They were eager to bring justice to their neighborhood. The young men involved were shortly linked to Mr. Thomas. Despite the growing number of years that Fred faced, none of it could change the events which had occurred.*

*"It's not fair. How do we go from wedding arrangements to funeral arrangements?" Gwen had said.*

*None of it was fair. It had only taken one afternoon to reverse a day that offered so much promise. Charlene's life, although short-lived, was the base of her father's world. Years of disputes and friction between the two of them had placed strains on their relationship. The separation in her last days weighed on him heavily. The guilt of not being there when she needed him the most struck him the hardest. Because of his difficulty handling Charlene's death, Jacquelyn and Carol mainly took care of the funeral arrangements.*

*Both men in Charlene's life dealt with her passing in their own ways, but Mr. Brown and Deon's troubles were rooted in remorse. Her father wished that he'd spent more time loving her and less time resenting her. They tried to escape the regret that tormented them by resolving Charlene's murder. Unfortunately, the mother Charlene had fought so hard to find was also lost in the tragedy. Mrs. Brown intended to continue to nurture the relationship that she and her daughter had begun to redevelop. She could have never imagined the one person who helped bring her child back to her would also be responsible for taking her away. However, the irony is that Fred also helped tear Mrs. Brown away from her family in the first place. Both mother and daughter had fought so hard for one another, only to lose one another yet again. Deon and Mr. and Mrs. Brown each felt the guilt of Charlene's loss hit at once, but the pain of the loss was different in each of their lives. The only hope that they grasped was the baby that was left behind.*

*Jacquelyn read the last entry in her Grandmother's Diary three times before closing the book. It was small, yet, it reached the core of her feelings. Just as her courtship with Will and her career flourished, her old life had to end. Deon's new family ended—or it was at least broken—as quickly as it* had started. Their union, in a sense, was the beginning of the end.

Jacquelyn rubbed her eyes and exhaled. From the time of the bakery shooting, rest was another casualty in their household. Everyone was affected by it in one way or another. Chris began to have several bed wettings throughout the night. His parents knew that it resulted from nightmares from the shooting. Ray was convinced that therapy was the way. He suggested taking him to a psychiatrist or, at least, speaking with someone from the church. Lena went further, saying,

"I think it would do the rest of us some good to shed some light on our darkness. We can't go on ignoring what's happened."

At first, Gwen refused, saying,

"I don't want anyone prying into my personal life and messing with my child's head." But her opinion quickly changed after being soaked from one of Chris' late-night bed wettings. She saw that this wasn't an issue they could rebound from without further help. The trauma wouldn't just go away.

Deon's late nights were taken over by bottle feedings and diaper changes. He now occupied his old room with Tori. In a few days, he would be leaving town. He had decided to join the military. He felt the best way he could change his daughter's life was if he changed his life first. He was still determining if his path was right for him. However, when it was all said and done, he wanted it to be a path his little girl could be proud of. Until his departure, he wanted to be with his daughter every minute that he could.

Jacquelyn came to herself shuffling around photos and books, trying to make a comfortable spot on her Grandmother's bed. Maybe after her nap, she would confront the reality that had flung itself upon her. She couldn't rely on the past to wash over the present. The good thing about the past is sometimes, in our minds, certain memories get hazy and begin to blur. With the present, there's no shield to protect us from what is. She closed her eyes and allowed her tense body to unwind on Lena's worn mattress. Before she could drift off to sleep, she felt someone watching her. She opened her eyes wide enough to see her Grandmother in the room's doorway. No use in acting like I'm sleeping. She knows me too well anyway, thought Jacquelyn. She sat up as Lena came over to sit next to her.

"How are you?" asked Lena.

"Right now, I don't think there's a word that exists to describe it. I know I should have stayed. Deon and the Browns have to be feeling a lot worse than me, but I couldn't take it. I had to get away from it all for a minute. With everybody feeling bad for you, it makes you feel helpless. You know I hate that feeling more than anything," said Jacquelyn.

"You're not helpless. I know things have been hectic, but we need you, Queen. If you allow yourself to see it, you'll know *it's also okay to rely on us too," she said, patting Jacquelyn's back. She then continued,*

*"Have you decided what you're going to do concerning Victoria?"*

*"Everything seems to be coming at me all at once. I think about you and Grandpa, and the way you took us in without a second thought. I don't know how things would've turned out if it weren't for this home. What if I can't do that for her if that responsibility is placed on me?"*

*"Queen, your brother asked you to be his baby girl's guardian because he knows what you're capable of."*

*"Okay...but how do I take on the role that was meant for the two of them?"*

*"You're making it sound like you're incompetent. Look, honey, if Mr. Brown could manage to raise a beautiful person like Charlene, I know that you're more than capable of doing the same if need be. After speaking about what's happened, Deon was determined to put in a plan for his daughter should something happen to him. Lining up the appropriate legal guardian was number one on his list. This is the most responsible thing I've seen him do. Don't take that wish away from him. He did not want to risk having his child placed in the wrong hands. God forbid something happens you know Victoria could not go through being raised with either Brown. Charlene's mother even supports his decision."*

*Jacquelyn knew that ultimately her only answer would be yes, but the weight of the responsibility delayed her from signing the papers. Jacquelyn hadn't held her niece since the passing of the infant's mother. Not that she purposely* shunned her, but every peep that the baby made was tended to by Deon or Gwen. Jacquelyn assumed her brother's first choice would be Gwen because she was already a mother and she adored her great niece.

"Why do you think he didn't choose Uncle Ray and Aunt Gwen? They're parents already, so they would make a better fit, right?"

"Gwen and Ray, at this point, you and I both know that would not be the best decision. They've just made peace in their marriage. Your brother knows best in this situation, it seems. Deep down we both know that. Anyway, you need to eat. I don't think I've seen you place a single piece of food in your mouth all day or yesterday. I can't have you starving over here," said Lena as she and Queen left the room. Jacquelyn passed the nursery and paused. Her Aunt was holding Victoria in the rocking chair. She spoke to the infant lovingly.

"You know you are very lucky. Yes, you are. Look at you looking just like your favorite auntie in the whole world," she said in a cooing voice.

"Yeah, she does look like me," said Jacquelyn teasing her Aunt.

"I was referring to her other favorite, but you look like me too, so consider yourself a lucky girl too."

"You're getting comfortable with this," said Jacquelyn.

"What?"

"You look like you're ready to add just one more," she said, pointing to Jessica in her arms.

"Actually, I wouldn't mind doing this again. I've always wanted to have another baby."

"Does Uncle Ray know about your special plans?"

"He will soon," said Gwen winking with a sly smile.

"Have you gotten anything to eat? If you want, I can watch her if you need to grab a bite," offered Jacquelyn.

"Thanks, but no thanks. Honey, I can do without half of those people in the front with their phony behinds. I haven't seen the majority of them since the last funeral. Most of them honestly are here for a free meal and gossip. They gave their condolences between a bite of chicken, and with the same breath, they're saying how much of a shame Deon has brought on our family or how certain ones ought to be ashamed for even showing up. I know the dirt on the very ones talking. If they knew what I know, ninety percent of *those lips would be sealed. Others are coming here, bragging about their kids, new cars, husbands, and wives. This is no show and tell cause if it was baby, I'd sure be telling!"*

*"It's funny how your own family can be. Most of them come in here with their noses up in the sky. The real shame is the only time that we see our relatives is at a funeral, wedding, or maybe the occasional reunion."*

*"I'm just grateful for the ten percent of the genuine ones. If it weren't for them, I'd tell the rest of them where to go. And that small percentage is mostly filled with folks pushing the six feet mark and hanging on by a thread. Maybe I'll get my chance sooner than later," she laughed. She caught herself after laughing too loudly. Jacquelyn caught herself, feeling*

embarrassed for exhibiting any emotion outside of her sadness.

"It's okay. If we didn't laugh, we'd be balled up, pulling our hair out in a corner somewhere."

"Yes, and you know that wouldn't be a good look," she said, flipping her hair. Then, she changed the pace of the conversation. "Where's Will?"

"After he brought me home, he went to the airport. He's been putting the trip off for me. He'll only be gone for two days. I told him to go. He can't spend all of his time babysitting me."

"I'm sure he doesn't look at it that way," said her Aunt.

"Well, before he does begin to look at it that way, I want to nip it in the bud. I know he'll be back in a couple of days, but I miss him already."

"Young love," said Gwen.

"I can't imagine what Deon is going through. Just the thought of never being able to see Will again scares me. My brother has to actually live with that every second."

"Even with all the arguing Ray and I do, I wouldn't be able to function without him."

"I can't believe it. You must have had a few glasses I mean bottles, of wine today. Gwen is sharing her sensitive side."

"Nope, this is one hundred percent sober Gwen talking here. Well, maybe a hint or two of wine," she said with an empty giggle.

While they were enjoying their first moments without thinking about everything else that was taking place around *them, high and mighty cousin Renee passed the room. She entered halfway to give her input on the scene.*

*"You two! What kind of behavior is this while the family is grieving downstairs? You, especially Gwen, should know better," she scolded them, pointing her finger at the ladies. Gwen stood up, handing the baby to Jacquelyn as she assumed the position to fire back. However, Lena beat her to her chance.*

*"Excuse you," said Lena standing only an inch or two from Renee's face.*

*"Oh, Aunt Lena, I was just looking for the bathroom."*

*"You were looking for something, but it wasn't the bathroom. I heard what you said. Where do you get off saying anything and pointing fingers at my girls? And for your information, we are the family. The family has to keep it together every day without people like you pointing a finger when you haven't lifted a hand to help any of us out. The last time I saw you, we were at a family reunion five years ago. Not one call in between like the rest of them stumbling in here with crocodile tears. It's just a show for some of you. See yourself*

downstairs or, better yet, out of my house if you can't keep your mouth shut!"

Renee squeaked out, "I'm sorry," as she swiftly walked away, trying to hide her first authentic tears from the time she had arrived.

"Maybe Grandma was the one who took an extra sip with you," whispered Jacquelyn. Lena sighed and came into the room.

"That's where I get it from. I was about to throw her out too. I normally say all the things that people in this house don't. I'm proud of you, Mama."

"Baby, I'm just tired of everyone pretending we're so close. I think there's a reason why I haven't seen a lot of them in years. Lord, that's terrible," said Lena.

"No, it's not terrible it's the truth. I think that's what we need around here. Truthfully I'm ready for them to leave, but I'm guessing you knew that already," said Gwen to her mother. Lena eventually went back downstairs to tend to the rest of the guests. Renee made sure to steer clear of her Aunt. Gwen stuck to her word and stayed upstairs with baby Victoria. If she had entertained the rest of the visitors, her main objective would be to go after Renee. The men of the house went out of their way to ensure each individual was comfortable and welcome, even if they were only partially welcome. They didn't allow pride or hard feelings to influence their attitudes. Although bad blood had been exchanged among many of the relatives over the years, the passing of a loved one drew that ten percent to wave the white flag. Nothing was sacred to that other large fraction, *whether it be kin or foe. Nevertheless, this latest passing marked a milestone amongst the Harts. Jacquelyn was obligated to temporarily assume the ranks as the head of Deon's family.*

*Chapter 16*

*The days of Deon's time at home began to dwindle away. This new and unwanted reality began to consume him. He overworked himself at Ray's limo service and tried to play super-dad when he returned home. Nothing, not even his little girl, could distract him from her mother's absence. On the day that Deon was to leave, Jacquelyn opened up, saying,*

*"I didn't forget about Tori's papers. Sorry about taking my time—."*

*"Stalling," Deon said, interrupting.*

*"Okay, stalling, but I signed them this morning. You know I was gonna sign them eventually, though."*

*"The only time you take your time is when you're afraid."*

*"Afraid? What should I be afraid of? She's just a baby. I just think of it as babysitting for a really long time. He laughed, "If that helps, okay." Jacquelyn enjoyed seeing her brother smile. It was a break from his recent somber demeanor.*

*"How have you been sleeping?" she asked.*

*"Surprisingly a lot better than I was. I thought sleeping in here, you know, would be weird without Charlene. My mind tended to play games with me, but I found more peace here than in my old room. Plus, baby girl and I have developed a*

system, a bottle at midnight, diaper change, and special lullaby around two."

"Do you think I'll have to move in here too?"

"No. You may wanna brush up on your singing skills. I hear you when I pass by the bathroom. Yeah, keep that on the other side of the shower."

"I'm sure she'll appreciate my talent," said Jacquelyn laughing. Victoria broke in with a loud whine. They both reached for her, but Deon allowed his sister to take charge. He watched her as she calmed the baby, rubbing her back and whispering softly.

"Another reason why I chose you," he said. She looked up to respond, but he continued.

"I know you've been wondering why I didn't choose Aunt Gwen or even Grandma. Aunt Gwen is a good mother, but that's not what she needs right now. I didn't choose Grandma because she's already done her job twice. She shouldn't have to pick up my slack. I mean, you shouldn't either."

"I think I know what you're saying."

"You've always taken care of me. In my mind, you've always been grown, even when we were kids, and you were about eight going on twenty-eight. I know you'll do the same for her," he said, kissing his daughter's cheek.

"Uncle Ray keeps telling me not to worry."

"Are you taking his advice?"

"Queen, how can I? Right now, Charlene and I are supposed to be raising our baby together. Instead, I can't help but worry about what I've done and how I have to face my baby *and answer questions I barely understand one day. I have to explain to her why she doesn't have a mother. That weight is on me and nobody else," he said, again becoming serious.*

*"And the rest of us will help you find those answers. Deon, I'm not in your position, and it's easy for me to say yes, it will work out, but I've learned that everything doesn't have to be on you. You lost the love of your life. No one gets over that in a couple of weeks. We don't expect that from you. My point is you aren't in this alone," said Jacquelyn.*

*"That's what Mr. Brown keeps telling me. I don't think I can talk to him, though."*

*"Mr. Brown lost a daughter, and I'm sure he can relate. He lost a wife. I think it would help to talk to him, not just because he's your baby's grandfather."*

*"We'll see," he said. Then, trying to ease the tension quickly rising, Deon changed the subject. "Grandma's biscuits are calling my name, and that's the only thing I wanna hear right now."*

*Lena prepared a special brunch. She made sure to invite Will and Mr. Brown. Will still refused to allow Deon to pay for his attorney's services. "Just consider it as a favor. You can return the favor by being my best man when you get home." Everyone there promised Deon that there would be no tears when he left, but Gwen was the first one to break. When he kissed his grandmother and hugged the others, he held his daughter for a few moments. She had been napping and then opened her eyes briefly while her father held her. Before he* could shed tears, he passed her to his sister. "Be good for Aunt Queen," he said as he let go of her little hand.

"I'll follow your routine," said Jacquelyn. Ray and Will accompanied Deon to the bus station. After her brother had gone, Jacquelyn went to her room, finding a box waiting for her. It was beautifully wrapped with a big red bow. She opened the box to find a black diary with her name engraved on the front. The first page had writing on it already. The message read:

Hey Jacquelyn,

I was searching for the right gift for you, and Grandma suggested this. You're giving me a gift I could never repay because you're giving my little girl a home. I know you'd never try to replace her mother, so in honor of Charlene's wishes I'd like you to be Victoria's godmother. You deserve that title, and I'm grateful we both have you in our lives. Thanks for knowing when to step in. I'm sure Will is going to take care for you while you're looking out for the rest of the family. If it's not too much of a hassle, take care of my car. Don't let Mr. Brown put any "baseball" sized dents in it. I love you, Queen.

Later,

Deon

P.S. Mom and Dad must be proud of you. Thanks for being the Queen of the Harts.

Deon's present would be well-spent. Jacquelyn wrote in it almost every day. As she watched her niece grow, she documented each new stage in the diary. Her motivation was *her brother. She planned on returning the book to him so he could catch up on each day that he couldn't be a part of.*

*Dear Diary, Deon only has four months left till he comes home to visit. We're all anxious about his return, but no one is as anxious as a certain little person. Every time Tori sees her daddy's picture, she smiles and points. Will and I finally set a wedding date. We plan on keeping it this time without rearranging it again. My brother still plans on being Will's best man. Gwen got her wish. She and Uncle Ray adopted a little girl a few months ago, and Chris the sweetest big brother. Uncle Ray is giving me away at my wedding, and Gwen will be my matron of honor. The two of them finally moved their family into their new home. They're right down the street, so she won't have to travel too far to boss us around. Grandma didn't hold any hard feelings against me for reading her diary. She says I needed a peek to gain some insight. She was right.*

*I'm working on getting Tori to say Queen, but for now, I'll settle for a smile. I'm glad we found one another.*

www.ingramcontent.com/pod-product-compliance
Lightning Source LLC
Chambersburg PA
CBHW061528120726
48001CB00004B/1446